Building Contract Litigation

nb.   supp. inside back cover.
2nd Edn 1985 ↗
  plus 029 r 10
      NRHA r Crouch.

Building Contract Litigation

Robert Fenwick Elliott
Solicitor

Oyez Longman

Oyez Longman Publishing Limited,
21/27 Lamb's Conduit Street
London WC1N 3NJ

ISBN 0 85120 601 8

First published 1981
Reprinted 1983

Set in Times and Univers by
Vantage Photosetting Co. Ltd.,
Eastleigh and London
and printed in Great Britain by
Biddles Ltd, Guildford, Surrey

Contents

Preface

Most general practitioners in the law become involved from time to time in building contract disputes. Sometimes these disputes are resolved in correspondence or in straightforward litigation in the county court. Sometimes, however, they are more complex, and the general practitioner can be at a disadvantage when an opponent is a specialist in this field. The purpose of this book is to provide a practical guide to building contract litigation and arbitration for the general practitioner.

All references to court rules are to the Rules of the Supreme Court. With the notable exception of Order 14 (which is of particular importance in building contract matters), similar principles are to be found in the County Court Rules. Likewise, references to practice and procedure relate to practice and procedure in the central office of the High Court, and it is left to the reader to rely upon his own experience of the practice of district registries.   *

As this book is concerned with the practical aspects of conducting building contract litigation and arbitration, its references to the law are intended to be guidelines rather than complete statements. For the latter the reader must refer to the established textbooks listed in Chapter 19 and to the Law Reports.

As from 1 October 1980, radical changes as to the making of orders for interim payment under Order 29, Part II, have come into effect. These new provisions are discussed at p 106. At the time of writing it is too early to gauge accurately what effect these new provisions will have upon building contract litigation, and the whole of this book must be read subject to the possibility that Order 29, Part II, will acquire a central role.

I am deeply indebted to the Official Referees Department at the Royal Courts of Justice, the Royal Institute of British Architects, the International Chamber of Commerce, the Contractors' Plant Association and those other individuals and organisations who have given me the benefit of their comments on the manuscript and permission to publish extracts from their materials.

Robert Fenwick Elliott
Manfield House
Strand, London WC2
February 1981

Table of Cases

TABLE OF CASES

Table of Statutes

Table of Rules

References

BLR

Building Law Reports, edited by Humphrey Lloyd QC and Colin Reese George Godwin Limited

Hudson

Hudson's Building and Engineering Contracts, by IN Duncan Wallace QC (10th Edition, 1970) Sweet & Maxwell; as amended by the First Supplement (1979)

Keating

Building Contracts, by Donald Keating QC (4th Edition, 1978) *
Sweet & Maxwell

JCT Contract

The JCT Standard Form of Building Contract 1980 Edition, Local Authorities Edition with quantities

The architect as arbitrator

The architect as arbitrator (1978 Edition), Royal Institute of British Architects prepared by LWM Alexander, Norman Royce and AB Waters

*Denotes the need to refer to the supplement to the first edition

Chapter 1

Forms of Contract

There are a variety of contractual or quasi-contractual bases upon which contractors carry out building work. These bases can be fundamentally different as to the principal obligations of the parties (ie the obligation on the contractor to do the work properly and the obligation on the employer to pay). Many of the day-to-day matters concerning the contract proceed more or less regardless of the form of contract, but it is impossible to obtain any clear view as to the legal position concerning a building contract without first understanding the basis of the contractual relationship in question. So beguiling can the use of familiar expressions be that it is by no means unknown for substantial building contract litigation to reach, or nearly reach, trial pleaded upon an entirely inappropriate basis. An error of that sort can change building contract litigation from mildly tedious into a positive nightmare.

It would be impossible, and in any event beyond the scope of this book, to set out a comprehensive classification of building contracts. There are, however, certain major features which are fundamental both to the method of payment (where the main contrast is between lump-sum contracts and cost contracts) and to the obligations of the builder (where much depends upon the extent to which the contractor undertakes any design obligation).

There follows a brief classification of the sorts of contract most commonly in use and a survey of some of the standard forms commonly used. Neither is exhaustive.

1 The classification of contracts

(a) Lump-sum contracts

A lump-sum contract is a contract whereby the contractor agrees for a pre-agreed price to execute certain defined building works. In principle, the contract is very simple but in practice there are many complicating factors.

The general rule in ordinary lump-sum contracts is that the contractor is entitled to be paid the pre-agreed lump sum as and when he substantially completes the work (*Hoenig* v *Isaacs* [1952] 2 All ER 176). Substantial completion does not necessarily entail the perfect execution of every detail of the works, and if the contractor is guilty of only comparatively minor defects and/or omissions then he is entitled to be paid the lump sum less a set-off in respect of his failings. In exceptional cases the parties may by clear words enter into an entire contract, which is 'an indivisible contract, one where the entire fulfilment of the promise by either party is a condition precedent to the right to call for the fulfilment of any part of the promise by the other' (*Hudson's Building Contracts*, 7th Ed; p 165). In these very exceptional circumstances the contractor is not entitled to be paid anything unless he completes the works without any defects or omissions at all.

Where there has been a failure by the contractor to achieve substantial completion (or, in the exceptional case, entire completion) then it may be possible for the employer to deny that the contractor is entitled to any payment at all. This is, however, swimming against the tide and the courts are most reluctant to see a contractor receive no payment at all for work that the contractor has done. As Lord Denning said in *Hoenig* v *Isaacs* at p 180: 'When a contract provides for a specific sum to be paid on completion of specified work, the courts lean against a construction of the contract which would deprive the contractor of any payment at all simply because there are some defects or omissions.'

The parties might arrive at the lump sum in one of a number of ways. Very often, the contractor places a price against each item in a bill of quantities or specification describing the works to be done on an item by item basis. The total is often subject to additions for overheads and profit, and to negotiation one way or the other. All this is irrelevant to the basic entitlement of the contractor, ie to the lump sum.

Although the lump sum is always the starting point, it is comparatively rare for the price the contractor is entitled to receive at the end of the day to be exactly the same as the lump sum. The lump sum is usually subject to adjustment for extra work, fluctuations, sub-contractors, and so on; a description of the more common adjustments appears at p 35 et seq. The lump sum is, however, the starting point for calculating the final entitlement.

(b) Cost contracts

Cost contracts manifest themselves under many different titles. They are known as cost contracts, cost-plus contracts, prime-cost contracts, or fee contracts. They are a species of measurement and value contracts, and some cost contracts are described as management contracts.

The basis of payment for the works under a cost contract is not any pre-agreed lump sum but the actual cost (or prime cost) of the works as performed. There is a term (implied if not expressed) in cost contracts that the contractor will perform the works efficiently and not wastefully, but subject to that the contractor is entitled to be paid whatever the work actually cost him. In addition, the contractor is almost always entitled to an additional payment, sometimes described as a fee, to cover his overheads and profit.

Particular care should be exercised with regard to estimates in cost contracts. These estimates are sometimes reproduced in the formal contract document and can have a contractual significance. They should however be rigidly distinguished from lump sums. Confusion particularly arises in the case of small informal building contracts where the contractor gives an estimate for the works. Whether he can be held to that estimate, or whether he can say that the job cost more than he anticipated, depends upon whether the contract is a lump-sum contract or a cost contract.

Many small informal contracts are cost contracts. In the case of more substantial works, however, cost contracting has always been less common than contracting on a lump-sum basis but cost contracting has remained a steady minority preference.

(c) Lump-sum contracts and cost contracts compared

The fundamental difference as to payment between lump-sum contracts and cost contracts leads to a number of differences between the detailed clauses.

It is fundamental to lump-sum contracts that the contract price is agreed at the time of the formation of the contract, which is usually at about the time of the commencement of work. The price in the case of cost contracts, on the other hand, cannot be ascertained until the works are complete and the cost calculated, and so of course the price cannot appear in the contract documents.

In the case of lump-sum contracts, the precise extent of the work needs to be defined with some care, otherwise it would not be possible to know how much work the contractor has to do for the pre-agreed price. In the case of costs contracts, on the other hand, precise definition of the contract work is of less importance because the price is dependent upon the amount of work that the contractor actually does. Lump-sum contracts usually contain a provision (and sometimes a complex formula) to fix the price of any extra work that may be ordered by the employer after the contract is formed. There is no need for this in a cost contract, where the contractor is paid in the same way for both original contract work and extras.

In the case of a lump-sum contract the contractor stands to gain or lose substantial sums of money according to the accuracy of his estimating. If the works are unexpectedly difficult, or if there is an unexpected rise in the cost of labour or materials, or if the charges of sub-contractors are unexpectedly high, then a lump-sum contractor must bear the cost and, unless there is express provision in the contract, is entitled only to the pre-agreed lump sum. In order to pass some of the burden of these risks from the contractor's shoulders to the employer's, sophisticated lump-sum contracts such as the standard JCT contract contain complex clauses designed to adjust the lump sum in certain circumstances. In particular, there are often fluctuations clauses, extremely complicated clauses as to the payment for the work of nominated sub-contractors, and far-reaching clauses as to the payment of loss and expense to the contractor in certain circumstances. All these clauses are unnecessary in a cost contract since (subject to his obligation to perform the works efficiently and not wastefully) the contractor is indemnified against whatever the cost of the works turns out to be.

Cost contracts usually contain a precise definition of what cost is recoverable by the contractor directly (these costs are called either prime cost or actual cost) and what cost the contractor is expected to recover within the fee or percentage addition. Typically, definitions of prime cost include all the cost of labour, materials and sub-contractors and other costs incurred on the site but exclude head office and administrative costs. Such a definition of prime cost is unnecessary in a lump-sum contract, although it can form part of the formula for the valuation of extras, as in clause 13.5.4 of the JCT contract.

There are other features of formal building contracts that are common to typical lump-sum contracts and to typical cost contracts. In particular, both forms of contract usually contain provisions as to when the contractor must complete the works, for extension of time in certain circumstances, for liquidated damages in the event of delay, for certification of interim and final payments due, as to determination of the contract by either party, as to retention of sums due and as to insurance.

(d) Re-measurement contracts

Re-measurement contracts are a sort of hybrid between lump-sum contracts and cost contracts. In re-measurement contracts the parties do not pre-agree any price for the work as a whole, but they do pre-agree the rates of remuneration to which the contractor shall be entitled. These rates can either be by reference to the amount of work that is done (eg so much per brick laid) or by reference to the amount of labour and materials expended (eg so much per hour for labourers).

Re-measurement contracts are sometimes easily recognisable, particularly where they are described as day-works contracts or are in the JCT form of contract with approximate quantities. They are sometimes less easy to recognise where, for example, the parties change what would otherwise be a lump-sum contract into a re-measurement contract by the use of the words 'all works are subject to re-measurement on completion'.

(e) Design-and-build contracts

The traditional system for substantial building works is that the employer causes the work to be designed by professional men and enters into a contract with a contractor to execute that design. Increasingly, however, contractors enter into contracts not only to build the works but also to design them.

The obligations of the contractor where he designs the works as well as builds them are obviously different from his obligations where the works are designed by a professional agent of the employer. In particular, the design-and-build contractor is usually absolutely liable on his promise that the works will be fit for their intended purpose; this is capable of arising by implication if not expressly (*Independent Broadcasting Authority* v *EMI Electronics Limited* (1981) 14 BLR 1). This contrasts with the position under the traditional system where the professional designers promise only to use reasonable care in the design.

Design-and-build contracts may be either lump-sum contracts or cost contracts. The cost arrangement is, however, often preferable both from the contractor's point of view (because he is unable to estimate exactly the cost of executing a design that is usually incomplete at the time the contract is made) and from the employer's point of view (because he would otherwise be especially vulnerable to the danger of the contractor cutting corners). Design-and-build contracts are often also regarded as particularly suitable for target arrangements, and there are a variety of sophisticated provisions as to payment.

Equally, very minor works where no professional designer is involved are frequently carried out under informal design-and-build contracts, although they are not usually described as such by the parties at the time of the formation of an informal contract.

2 The standard forms

There are a number of forms of building contract in standard use. In the centre of the range of the standard forms is the JCT contract in its six current versions, each of which runs to some 40,000 words and is designed for use with the standard form of sub-contract (which runs to some 30,000 words).

(a) The Joint Contracts Tribunal

The JCT is a body whose constituents are the Royal Institute of British Architects, the National Federation of Building Trades Employers, the Royal Institution of Chartered Surveyors, the Association of County Councils, the Association of Metropolitan Authorities, the Association of District Councils, the Greater London Council, the Committee of Associations of Specialist Engineering Contractors, the Federation of Associations of Specialists and Sub-contractors, the Association of Consulting Engineers and the Scottish Building Contract Committee. The JCT publish not only the Standard Form of Building Contract (in six versions) but also a series of documents designed for use with the main contract, an Agreement for Minor Building Works and a Fixed Fee Form of Prime Cost Contract.

The JCT contracts are published by RIBA Publications Ltd and can be obtained from the RIBA bookshop, 66 Portland Place, London W1N 4AD, or by mail order from RIBA Publications Limited, Finsbury Mission, Moreland Street, London EC1V 9VB, tel 01–251 0791.

(b) The JCT Standard Form of Building Contract 1980 Edition

This contract is the latest in a long line that stretches back into the nineteenth century. For many years the Royal Institute of British Architects published the contract, and it was popularly known as the RIBA Contract. Now the RIBA is only one of the constituent bodies of the JCT. The contract comes in six versions: Private With Quantities; Private Without Quantities; Private With Approximate Quantities; Local Authorities With Quantities; Local Authorities Without Quantities; and Local Authorities With Approximate Quantities.

The versions 'With Quantities' and 'Without Quantities' are lump-sum contracts. The lump-sum is stated in the Articles at the beginning of the contract, but it is subject to adjustment for many things.

The editions 'With Approximate Quantities' are not lump-sum contracts at all, but are re-measurement contracts. They achieve this end by deleting all references to the contract sum and extending the application of the valuation of variations clause in the lump-sum contract to the whole of the works.

The 1980 edition of the contract has re-numbered the clauses from the previous 1963 edition and has made a number of changes. Some of the major features of the JCT form are as follows. The comments apply to the edition 'With Quantities'.

Article 2—This sets out the lump sum, which is referred to in the contract as 'the Contract Sum'.

Article 3—This names the architect, who not only has power to issue instructions as to various matters which the contractor is obliged to follow but also has the power and indeed the duty to issue certificates which are binding upon the parties unless and until they are reviewed in litigation or arbitration. The more important certificates determine the amount due to the contractor as the works proceed (Clause 30.1.1), the amount due at the conclusion of the contract (Clause 30.8) and as to what extension of time if any the contractor is entitled (Clause 25).

Article 4—This names the quantity surveyor whose essential function is to advise the architect as to the value of work done by the contractor.

Article 5—This is a wide-reaching arbitration clause.

Clause 1—This is the interpretation and definition clause.

Clause 2—This shows that the contractor's obligation is to carry out and complete the works shown on the contract drawings and other contract documents; there is no obligation on the contractor as to the efficacy of the design.

Clause 13.2—This empowers the architect to issue instructions requiring a variation to the work. Despite the width of the words used it is suggested in *Keating* that 'he has no authority to vary or waive the conditions of contract, nor to vary the whole nature of the works, for example, to change works designed as a single dwelling-house into a complex block of flats. He probably cannot omit work in order to have it carried out by another contractor.'.

Clause 13.5—This sub-clause sets out the rules for the payment for variations and extra work. In broad terms, the rules provide for extrapolation from the bills of quantities if possible; if this is not possible variations are valued at cost. The importance of the valuation rules can be over-estimated, since if they do not reimburse the contractor the direct loss and/or expense incurred by the contractor by reason of the variation, then the contractor can apply under Clause 26.1 for ascertainment (and hence payment; Clause 26.5) of such loss and expense. In other words the Clause 26 'tops up' the valuation rules in Clause 13.5.

Clause 17.1—This provides that the architect shall certify the date of Practical Completion. Unless and until that certificate is overturned in arbitration or litigation, it is conclusive.

Clause 17.3—After Practical Completion there is a Defects Liability Period (usually but not necessarily six months) and the architect may require the contractor to make good any defects appearing within that time. The contractor does not get paid for this.

Clause 19.2—The contractor needs the written consent of the architect (not to be unreasonably withheld) before sub-contracting any part of the works. This requirement is frequently ignored and does not necessarily affect the contractor's right to payment.

Clause 24.2.1—This is the liquidated damages clause, whereby the employer may recover liquidated damages at whatever rate is set out in the appendix to the contract if the architect certifies that the contractor has failed to complete the works by the Completion Date.

Clause 25—The 'Completion Date' as defined in the 1980 edition can be varied; the architect must revise the Completion Date if the contractor is delayed by a 'Relevant Event'. The Relevant Events include such matters as bad weather, strikes, extra work being ordered, being delayed by the architect's lateness in providing necessary instructions and delay on the part of nominated sub-contractors.

Clause 26—Delay usually cost both the employer and the contractor money. The point about the Relevant Events is that they *all* allow the contractor more time to complete the work; the contractor is relieved from paying the employer's liquidated damages. Clause 26 goes further in respect of *some* of the Relevant Events, in particular delay by the architect in providing necessary instructions (Clause 26.2.1) and extra work (Clause 26.2.7); it entitles the contractor to be re-imbursed his own loss and expense. The contractor may be entitled to loss and expense under Clause 26 not only if the works as a whole are delayed (prolongation) but also if the regular progress of any part of the works is materially affected (disruption). See p 42 as to the quantification of loss and expense.

Clauses 27 and 28—These clauses are the determination clauses, and although they are expressly without prejudice to any other rights or remedies of the parties they in effect codify within the contract the effect of what would otherwise be regarded as a repudiatory breach or frustrating event. In practice, it is far more common for a party to determine the contract under the express clauses than it is to rely on his common law right to accept repudiatory conduct as such, but it is frequently argued that the wrongful exercise of the determination clauses amounts itself to repudiation.

Clause 30.1—This clause provides for the architect to issue interim certificates, usually monthly, for payments on account to the contractor.

Clause 30.4—The employer retains 5% of whatever would otherwise be payable on interim certificates. Of this, 2½% is released to the contractor on Practical Completion, and the other 2½% is released when the architect certifies that the contractor has made good the defects appearing within the defects liability period.

Clause 30.6.2—This is the clause which sets out how much the contractor gets paid at the end of the day. The basic entitlement is to the contract sum but this is adjusted in a number of respects.

Clause 30.8—The Final Certificate is usually due about a year after Practical Completion. It sets out the final state of the account and confirms that the architect is satisfied with the work. It is unlike all the other certificates in that it is not subject to review in arbitration or litigation unless and to the extent that such arbitration or litigation is commenced within fourteen days after the certificate is issued.

Clause 35—This is the nominated sub-contractors' clause. It is extremely complicated, but the basic scheme is that in respect of certain parts of the work the architect reserves to himself (usually by the use of a prime-cost sum in the bills of quantities) the right of nomination. The contractor must (subject to certain limited rights of objection) then enter into a nominated sub-contract with whichever sub-contractor is chosen by the architect. Each interim certificate directs the contractor precisely how much to pay to each nominated sub-contractor, and the employer then pays the contractor that amount in respect of that work. The standard form of nominated sub-contract (NSC/4) is specifically designed to fit in with the nomination clause in the main contract, and under it the sub-contractors' entitlement to payment is fixed by the architect under the main contract. Contractors who are not nominated (domestic sub-contractors) are not subject to the nominated sub-contractor provisions.

Clauses 38, 39 and 40—These are the fluctuation clauses and are alternatives for the parties to choose. Each of them in its different way is designed to share between the employer and the contractor the effects of inflation. Clause 38 (which is the least generous to the contractor) allows the contractor to recover increases in taxes, etc. Clause 39 (which contains better protection for a contractor) also allows the contractor to recover increases in the cost of labour and materials by a complex set of rules related to increases in the wage rates agreed with the relevant unions and market prices of the relevant materials, goods, electricity and fuels. Clause 40 applies the formula rules issued by the JCT, which work on an index basis.

(c) JCT Nominated Sub-Contract NSC4

Prior to 1980 it was common for contractors and nominated sub-contractors to enter into sub-contracts in a form known as 'the Green Form', which was issued under the sanction of or approved by the National Federation of Building Trades Employers and other bodies. The Green Form is now out of date. There was a further contract ('the Blue Form') which was intended for use in domestic sub-contracts. The Blue Form remains in use.

In 1980 the JCT extended the range of standard forms by including documents for use in nominations. These were as follows:

NSC/1   Nominated Sub-Contract Tender and Agreement

NSC/2   Employer/Nominated Sub-Contractor Agreement for use where Sub-Contractor tendered on NSC/1

NSC/2a Employer/Nominated Sub-Contractor Agreement for use where Tender NSC/1 not used

NSC/3   Standard Form of Nomination of a Sub-Contractor where Tender NSC/1 has been used

NSC/4   Sub-Contract for sub-contractors who have tendered on Tender NSC/1 and executed Agreement NSC/2 and have been nominated by Nomination NSC/3

NSC/4a Sub-Contract NSC/4 adapted for use where Tender NSC/1, Agreement NSC/2 and Nomination NSC/3 have not been used.

The central document among these is NSC/4, which is the successor to the Green Form. This is an extremely complicated contract; it runs to about 30,000 words, bears a complex parasitic relationship to the main contract, and incorporates the tender document (NSC/1) by reference.

NSC/4 is either a lump-sum contract or a re-measurement contract according to how the tender form NSC/1 (if there is one) has been completed. There is an alternative on the tender form between a 'sub-contract sum', which leads to a lump-sum contract, and a 'tender sum', which leads to a re-measurement contract. If the parties choose the lump-sum arrangement, then the sub-contract sum is adjusted under Clause 21.10.2 in much the same way as under the main contract forms 'With Quantities' or 'Without Quantities'. If the re-measurement option is chosen, then the sub-contractors' final entitlement ('the Ascertained Final Sub-Contract Sum') is calculated under Clause 21.11.2 and does not necessarily bear any close relationship to the tender sum, the latter having little contractual significance.

The contractor's obligation as to payment is to pay the sub-contractors as and when the architect under the main contract so certifies. The intention is that the architect should in each interim certificate under the main contract direct the contractor as to what sum is to be payable to each of the nominated sub-contractors. The sub-contractor then has seventeen days from the date of the issue of each interim certificate to make payment to those sub-contractors, and provided he does so he may retain a cash discount of $2\frac{1}{2}\%$ (Clause 21.3.1.1.) As far as final payment of nominated sub-contractors is concerned, the architect has an obligation under Clause 35.16 of the main contract to certify practical completion of nominated sub-contract work, and must within a year after that certify the amount finally due to that sub-contractor (main contract Clause 35.17).

NSC/4 contains a time for completion (which is usually earlier than the time for completion under the main contract) and like the main contract contains many detailed clauses as to architects' instructions, insurance, determination, defects liability period, valuation of variations etc. It also contains a choice of fluctuations clauses, though it should be noted that it is by no means imperative that the fluctuations clause under a sub-contract must be in the same form as a fluctuations clause under the main contract; indeed it is quite common to have a fixed-price main contract with fluctuating sub-contracts, or vice versa.

It was said by the Court of Appeal in *Tersons Limited* v *Stevenage Development Corporation* [1965] 1 QB 37 that the Green Form was not to be construed contra proferentem against either the contractor or the sub-contractor, and the same will presumably go for NSC/4.

(d) ICE Conditions of Contract

A form of contract for civil engineering works is issued under the sponsorship and approval of the Institution of Civil Engineers, the Association of Consulting Engineers and the Federation of Civil Engineering Contractors. It occupies in the civil engineering world the central position occupied by the JCT contract in the building world. The current edition, the fifth, was issued in 1973.

The ICE Contract (Fifth Edition) is a re-measurement contract; see p 4. The engineer appointed under the contract has wide powers of certification and is probably in a more powerful position than the architect under the JCT contracts. The contract contains detailed provisions as to such matters as variations, nominated sub-contractors, determination, interim certification and many other matters.

The detailed wording of the ICE conditions differs from the JCT wording in practically every respect. There does not appear to be any logical reason for this and indeed the Banwell Report in 1974 recommended unification. Since that time both the ICE and the JCT have issued new editions, but neither makes any significant advance towards unification.

(e) CPA Conditions

When contractors require cranes, earth moving equipment and other plant they frequently hire it. The hiring is almost always in the terms or substantially in the terms of the Model Conditions for the Hiring of Plant (with effect from September 1979) which are the copyright of the Contractors' Plant Association, 28 Eccleston Street, London, SW1 (01–730 7117). The Model Conditions replace the General Conditions for Hiring of Plant previously issued by the CPA.

There are two noteworthy features of the CPA conditions. The first is that they pass much of the risk of damage to the hirer, including the risk of negligence on the part of a competent operator provided by the owner. Condition 8 provides as follows:

> 'When a driver or operator is supplied by the Owner with the plant, the Owner shall supply a person competent in operating the plant and such person shall be under the direction and control of the Hirer. Such drivers or operators shall for all purposes in connection with their employment in the working of the plant be regarded as the servants or agents of the Hirer (but without prejudice to any of the provisions of Clause 13) who alone shall be responsible for all claims in connection with the operation of the plant by the said drivers or operators. The Hirer shall not allow any other person to operate such plant without the Owner's previous consent to be confirmed in writing.'

Condition 13 provides as follows:

> '(a) For the avoidance of doubt it is hereby declared and agreed that nothing in this Clause affects the operation of Clauses 5, 8 and 9 of this Agreement
> (b) During the continuance of the hire period the Hirer shall subject to the provisions referred to in sub paragraph (a) make good to the Owner all loss of or damage to the plant from whatever cause the same may arise, fair wear and tear accepted, and except as provided in Clause 9 herein, and shall also fully and completely indemnify the Owner in respect of all claims by any person whatsoever for injury to person or property caused by or in connection with or arising out of the use of the plant and in respect of all costs and charges in connection therewith whether arising under statute or common law. In the event of loss of or damage to the plant, hire charges shall be continued at idle time rates until settlement has been effected.
> (c) Notwithstanding the above the Owner shall accept liability for damage, loss or injury due to or arising

(i) prior to delivery of any plant to the site of the hirer where the plant is in transit by transport of the Owner or as otherwise arranged by the Owner

(ii) during the erection of any plant, where such plant requires to be completely erected on site, always provided that such erection is under the exclusive control of the Owner or his Agent

(iii) during the dismantling of any plant, where plant requires to be dismantled after use prior to removal from site, always provided that such dismantling is under the exclusive control of the Owner or his Agent

(iv) after the plant has been removed from the site and is in transit on to the Owner by transport of the Owner or as otherwise arranged by the Owner

(v) where plant is travelling to or from a site under its own power with a driver supplied by the Owner.'

The effectiveness of the predecessors to these clauses was affirmed by the House of Lords in *Arthur White (Contractors) Ltd* v *Tarmac Civil Engineering Ltd* [1967] 1 WLR 1508. It will remain to be seen what effect the Unfair Contract Terms Act 1977 will have upon the Model Conditions, which are the result of several years' negotiations between the Contractors' Plant Association representing the plant hire industry, the Federation of Civil Engineering Contractors representing the main client industry of civil engineering and the Office of Fair Trading. The Model Conditions do bear a prominent notice on their face drawing the attention of the hirer to the need to insure against his liabilities under Clauses 8 and 13, and the courts may well take the view that the Model Conditions should be given their literal meaning as between commercial enterprises without the interference of the 1977 Act.

The other noteworthy point about the CPA conditions relates to their universality. It is clear from *British Crane Hire* v *Ipswich Plant Hire* [1974] 1 All ER 1059 that the courts will readily infer the incorporation of the CPA conditions as between commercial entities who regularly contract under such conditions.

A commentary on the Model Conditions appeared in the magazine *Contract Journal* on 3 January 1980 (p 37) and 10 January 1980 (p 22).

(f) Other standard forms

Traditionally, the JCT contract and its forerunner the RIBA contract have been by far the most widely used of the standard forms. Since the formation of the Joint Contract Tribunal, however, the form has consistently shown a tendency to grow in length and complexity; it has been pointed out that the contract has grown from seventeen pages in 1952, to thirty-three pages in 1963, and is now (with quantities) fifty-nine pages long but in smaller print. This tendency has created a reaction in the industry against the use of the form and it has yet to be seen whether and to what extent the JCT contract will retain its central position in the future. At the time of writing, the Association of Consultant Architects has indicated

* strong opposition to JCT 1980 and proposes to produce its own, much shorter, standard form of building contract.

The JCT has for some years also issued a four-page Agreement for Minor Building Works which is, in effect, a very much abbreviated version of the 1963 edition of the standard form. This form is designed for use where minor building works or maintenance works, for which a specification or specification and drawings have been prepared, are to be carried out for an agreed lump sum and where an architect/supervising officer has been appointed on behalf of the employer.

The Joint Contracts Tribunal also issue the Fixed Fee Form of Prime Cost Contract, which is a thirty-page cost contract which incorporates much of the wording of the 1963 edition of the standard form.

Where local authorities or regional health authorities instruct substantial building works, they usually do so under the Local Authorities Additions of the JCT Standard Form. Where central government is the employer, the form of contract is often the government's own form, GC/Works/1, which replaces their former form CC/Works/1.

In the case of contracts to be carried out overseas, whether they be building contracts or civil engineering contracts, the form used is often the FIDIC form prepared by the Fédération Internationale des Ingénieurs-Conseils and the Fédération Internationale Européenne de la Construction, and this contract shares many of the provisions of the ICE contract.

In addition to the above, there are a number of other standard contracts in current use that have been prepared by various professional bodies and by particular contractors and sub-contractors for their own use.

Chapter 2
Contractual Procedure

1 Design

The traditional starting point for an employer is to engage the services of an architect or a surveyor to design the required work. This design may be in many stages and commence with a feasibility study, but eventually the design is progressed into the form of detailed drawings which show precisely the required work. In due course these drawings are incorporated by reference into the contract between the employer and the contractor and represent the basic description of the work which the contractor is required to execute. The drawings are frequently amplified by one or more specifications and/or by sections of the bills of quantities.

The preparation of the design can take various forms, usually according to the magnitude of the project. In major building works for the construction or substantial alteration of buildings it is usual for the basic design to be in the hands of an architect. Detailed parts of the design are frequently delegated; for example the design of foundations and frame is frequently put in the hands of consulting or structural engineers and the design of heating and air conditioning installations is frequently entrusted to heating and ventilation engineers. The architect generally retains responsibility for co-ordinating the designs of these specialists. In medium-sized works, the whole of the design is frequently in the hands of a single architect or surveyor. In the case of small works, it is often the case that neither the employer nor any architect or surveyor employed by him does any of the design work, save to indicate the nature of the work he requires. Where, for example, an employer simply requires a road across his land he may merely indicate to the contractor that he requires a road along such a route suitable for such traffic. The design of the road is left to the contractor.

This last example is a simple example of a design-and-build contract. It is unusual for a design-and-build contract to give rise to any difficult questions as to design; the responsibility for ensuring that the work is effected properly rests squarely with the contractor and if defects appear it is irrelevant whether they are defects of design or of workmanship.

15

In the normal case of traditional contracts (ie where the design is not the responsibility of the contractor but that of the employer's architect) then much importance can attach to the question of whether a defect is a design defect or a defect of workmanship. It is impossible to lay down hard and fast rules as to whether any particular defect will be one or another, for the choice between a flat roof and a pitched roof will be a matter of design, but the choice between a screw and a nail may well be a matter of workmanship. As a rule of thumb, the shape, dimensions, choice of material and other matters apparent from the drawings are generally regarded as design matters and the things left over for the good sense of the contractor are generally regarded as matters of workmanship.

Sometimes an employer or his architect nominates a sub-contractor or supplier who offers more than mere workmanship. For example, where the works include a lift it is obvious that the manufacturer of the lift will design the lift installation. It is beyond the scope of this book to consider in detail the design liabilities of sub-contractors and suppliers, but in such an example the supplier of the lift would probably be liable to the employer if the lift had a design defect — either for breach of collateral warranty (as in *Shanklin Pier Co Ltd* v *Detel Products* [1951] 2 KB 854), which may have been reduced to a formal direct warranty agreement between the employer and the nominated sub-contractor as in the JCT form NSC/2, or for negligence (as in *Independent Broadcasting Authority* v *EMI Electronics Ltd* (1981) 14 BLR 1).

2 Bills of quantities

A bill of quantities is usually prepared by a quantity surveyor once the drawings have been prepared by the architect. The purpose of the bill of quantities is to set out in itemized form all the work that is shown by the drawings and the opportunity is usually taken also to describe in further detail what the contractor must do. The process of preparing bills of quantities from drawings is known as 'taking off'. In an effort to simplify and unify the method of description of works the Royal Institution of Chartered Surveyors and the National Federation of Building Trades Employers produce a book known as the Standard Method of Measurement of Building Works (usually abbreviated to the Standard Method of Measurement (SMM)) and it is normal for bills of quantities to be prepared in accordance with it. Clause 2.2.2.1. of the JCT Contract expressly so provides.

Once the bills of quantities have been prepared, copies of them are given to the contractor for the contractor to prepare his tender. The contractor goes through the bills of quantities item by item, placing against each item his price for that particular item of work. The contractor then totals all the items (often including an item for profit) and so arrives at the lump sum. The process of the contractor putting a price against each item is known as 'pricing' and a bill of quantities which has prices inserted (traditionally in a column on the right hand side of the page) is known as a 'priced bill of quantities'.

It is plain that in respect of original contract work the distribution of the lump sum among the items in the bills of quantities is irrelevant. The contractor's entitlement is to the lump sum, and it does not matter how he has arrived at it. There are, however, two particularly important consequences of the way in which the lump sum is distributed.

The first relates to the valuation of variations under the JCT system. Under Clause 13.5.1.1. there is a rule that 'where the (extra) work is of similar character to, is executed under similar conditions as, and does not significantly change the quantity of, work set out in the Contract Bills the rates and prices for the work so set out shall determine the valuation'. In other words, the price set against each individual item not only represents a part of the total lump sum, but also sets out the prima facie entitlement of the contractor where more of the same thing is ordered. Because of this it has been known for contractors to indulge in the entertaining but dangerous exercise known as 'loading'. When considering alternative tenders, the employer is interested in the total lump sum and not the breakdown of this as between the individual items. Accordingly, if a contractor upon receipt of the bills of quantities thinks that the employer is likely to require more, say, painting work then he sometimes 'loads' the painting rates and correspondingly reduces the rates for some other area of the work that he does not think will be increased. In this way, he hopes to be paid at a premium when the additional painting is ordered. If the contractor does this, however, he runs the risk that the employer might omit the painting and order more of the very sort of work that the contractor has underpriced.

Secondly, contractors sometimes indulge in what is known as 'front-end loading'. The contractor ups his rates for the initial work at the expense of his rates for the finishing work so that he receives a greater proportion of the eventual recovery in the early interim payments rather than the late interim payments.

3 Tenders

Once the architect has prepared the design, and the quantity surveyors have prepared the bills of quantities, and the contractors on the tendering list have priced those bills of quantities, then the contractors all submit their tender forms in sealed envelopes. These tenders are then all opened at the same time by the employer or his architect, and the employer enters into a contract with the successful tenderer. Ordinarily, there is no implication that a contractor is to be paid for his costs of preparing his tender *(William Lacey (Hounslow) Limited* v *Davis* [1957] 1 WLR 932).

The normal intention is that the hopeful contractors should prepare their tenders independently. Occasionally, however, tendering contractors 'take a cover'. This might occur where a contractor is not in a position because of his current work load to undertake a contract for which he has been invited to tender, and yet does not wish to be seen to turn work away. He therefore contracts a friendly contractor who is also tendering and pitches his own price a little higher than that other contractor's price. The taking of covers is of course carefully concealed from the employer. It should be noted in passing that agreements between contractors as to tendering are potentially within the scope of the Restrictive Trade Practices Act 1976.

Tenders should be distinguished from estimates. A tender is in the nature of an offer which is capable of acceptance in the legal sense. It is usually a document which incorporates a priced bill of quantities. The term estimate is used far more widely and can either represent an offer capable of acceptance so as to form a lump-sum contract or it can merely be the contractor's view as to the eventual claim he will make for payment under a cost contract or in quantum meruit. There is certainly no rule of law that the use of the word 'estimate' on a document prevents it amounting to an offer *(Croshaw* v *Pritchard* (1899) 16 TLR 45), and where such a document carries standard terms and conditions then that will generally be a strong indication that the document is an offer capable of giving rise to a contract if accepted expressly or by conduct. Estimates may of course take verbal form as well as written form.

The precise terms of estimates should be carefully considered to establish whether they constitute an offer or merely a view as to the likely cost. Even if the estimate is merely a view as to the likely cost, the contractor may be liable for its accuracy in misrepresentation, for breach of collateral warranty, or in negligence *(Esso* v *Mardon* [1976] QB 801).

4 Letters of intent

It can take a long time for the formalities of a substantial building contract to be concluded, and where the employer wishes the contractor to get started as soon as possible he sometimes sends a letter expressing his intention to enter into a formal contract in due course. Such letters are sometimes expressed to be 'subject to contract'.

Such a letter of intent is not usually regarded as capable of giving rise to a binding contract for the execution of the works as a whole. Where a contract is entered into in due course, then that contract may have retrospective effect (see *Trollope & Colls Limited* v *Atomic Power Constructions Limited* [1963] 1 WLR 333) and the letter of intent will ultimately have little effect. Where a contract is not entered into but the contractor has undertaken works, it seems that the court will lean towards a construction of a letter of intent that allows the contractor to be paid in respect of work done in reliance upon the letter of intent (*Turriff Construction Limited* v *Regalia Knitting Mills Limited* (1971) 9 BLR 20).

5 Contractual documents

Once the employer and contractor have reached agreement they usually embody that agreement in a number of contractual documents. The central document is the document usually referred to as 'the contract'. In the JCT form, it comprises the Articles of Agreement and the Conditions.

The contract itself does not usually describe the extent of the works in any detail. This description usually appears in the drawings and the bills of quantities, all of which are incorporated into the contract by reference.

6 Nomination

It frequently happens that the employer wishes to have certain parts of the works carried out not by the main contractor but by some other building company, often a specialist. The normal way for an employer to proceed in these circumstances in England is not for him to enter into parallel contracts with the builders but to engage a main contractor with a contract which provides that the main contractor must enter into sub-contracts with sub-contractors nominated by the employer. It is very common for sub-contractors to be nominated to perform heating and ventilation works, lift installation, window installation, steel frame construction and any other parts of building works which involve specialist building techniques or patented or unique building materials. Sometimes, the employer is interested in particular materials rather than particular workmanship and he may then nominate the supplier.

The term 'nomination' is used loosely to describe any instruction from an employer or his architect to a builder to enter into a contract with a nominated sub-contractor or supplier. The feature of a nominated sub-contract is that the main contractor simply does as he is told. It is the employer or the architect who enters into the negotiations with the intended nominated sub-contractor, and when those negotiations are at a stage when the employer is satisfied with the sub-contractor's tender then the main contractor is instructed to accept it. In theory, difficult questions of law as to purported acceptance of offers by persons other than the offeree can arise, but in practice nomination is widespread and a proposed nominated sub-contractor who addresses his tender to the architect will probably anticipate that the offer will be taken up by a main contractor he may never even have heard of.

7 Certification and interim payment

Where a contractor is involved in substantial building works, it is usually essential to him to receive payment for the works as they proceed. Most formal building contracts (including the JCT form) provide that the architect named in the contract should issue interim certificates as to the amount to be paid to the contractor month by month. The arbitration clause in the contract usually empowers the arbitrator to open up and review such certificates. Further, it is submitted in *Keating* (p 414) that 'ordinarily the Court will hold that the parties have impliedly agreed that the Court should have all the powers of the arbitrator under the Clause'. Unless and until a certificate is overruled in arbitration or litigation, it usually creates a debt from the employer to the contractor.

One major practical effect of interim certificates is that they are generally regarded as sufficient to entitle a contractor to judgment under Ord 14 unless the employer has a set-off (eg for defective work). Where the contractor has the benefit of a certificate duly given pursuant to a contractual provision, the court does not generally require any further proof that the money is due.

There was formerly a line of cases, commencing with the Court of Appeal decision in *Dawnays Ltd* v *FG Minter Ltd and Trollope and Colls Ltd* [1971] 1 WLR 1205, which held that cash was the life blood of the building industry and that certificates for payment were to be treated as in the nature of negotiable instruments— that is to say to be paid without any set-off except arising out of fraud. The 'no set-off' rule was overturned by the House of Lords in *Modern Engineering (Bristol) Ltd* v *Gilbert Ash (Northern) Ltd* [1974] AC 689, where it was held that building contracts were subject to the ordinary rule as to set-off. It remains the case, however, that the court will not be dissuaded from awarding judgment under Ord 14 where the defendant makes bare allegations as to defective work or some other cross-claim; the set-off must be properly detailed and quantified. See p 97.

Although the *Gilbert Ash* case is of importance as to the principle that ordinary rules of set-off apply to claims based on certificates for payment, it is of limited application upon its particular circumstances. The claim in the case was by a sub-contractor against a main contractor under a certificate issued under the main contract. The sub-contract was not, however, in the usual form (then the Green Form). If it had been in the usual form the contractor would only have been entitled to its set-off if the architect had issued a certificate as to the delay of the nominated sub-contractor under Clause 27(d) (ii) of the then current form, which now appears in a slightly modified form as Clause 35.15.1 (*Brightside Kilpatrick Engineering Services* v *Mitchell Construction (1973) Ltd* [1975] 2 Lloyd's Rep 483).

It is usual for the certifier under the contract to be the architect who has designed the works and he will remain the employer's agent for the purpose of such matters as issuing instructions. There are, however, many cases which show that when certifying the architect must act fairly and independently between the parties to the contract (in particular *Hickman & Co* v *Roberts* [1913] AC 299 HL and *Panamena Europea Navegacion* v *Leyland & Co Ltd* [1947] AC 428). The architect acts as the agent of the employer in all these matters, but his duty to his employer in certification is to act in a fair and professional manner (*Sutcliffe* v *Thackrah* [1974] AC 727 HL). The architect may be liable in negligence to the contractor if he fails to certify with due care (see *Arenson* v *Casson Beckman Rutley & Co* [1977] AC 405 HL).

There is usually a provision in a building contract also giving the architect the function of certifying what extensions of time are due to the contractor. Under the 1963 edition of the JCT form there was some doubt about the precise extent of the architect's right to make such certificates upon an interim basis, but under the 1980 edition there is express power for the architect to certify as to time on an interim basis. The same principles as to impartiality apply to such certification as apply to certification of interim payments.

8 Practical completion and defects liability periods

Building works, like the arrow of Eleatic paradox, have a propensity to get closer and closer to completion but never quite to arrive. The building industry has accordingly evolved the concept of practical completion, which in broad terms means the stage at which the works are reasonably ready for their intended use but notwithstanding that there may be some minor defects or omissions.

The date of practical completion is important in a number of respects. It is generally the date on which the works are deemed to be complete for the purpose of liquidated damages. It is usually the time at which the architect ceases to have power to vary the works and it ordinarily marks the commencement of the defects liability period.

The defects liability period is akin to a guarantee period and the contractor usually has the obligation, and indeed the right, to remedy defects appearing within this time. The contractor is usually required to remedy these defects free of charge but the practice is to the benefit of both parties since the contractor would otherwise be liable for the greater cost of another contractor remedying the defects.

Ordinarily, a provision for the making good of defects within a defects liability period does not deprive the employer of his damages for defects appearing outside that period (*Hancock and Others v B W Anerley Brazier Ltd* [1966] WLR 1316). In the JCT form, the time for issue of the final certificate (whereby the architect certifies that the works are satisfactory) is fixed by reference to the certificate of completion of making good defects (Clause 30.8) but there is no attempt to limit the contractor's liability to the defects that appear within the defects liability period. If a contractor were to seek such a limit to his liability in the contract he may well be thwarted by the Unfair Contract Terms Act 1977.

9 The final account

The final account, as its name suggests, is the document which shows the total price eventually to be paid for the works. A positive final account is one which shows a further sum due to the contractor; a negative final account is one which shows that the contractor has been overpaid through the interim payments. Although the expression final account is not expressly used in the JCT contract, it is colloquially used to describe the computation referred to in Clause 30.6.3.

Chapter 3
Terms of the Contract

1 Express terms

Sometimes there is a formal agreement entered into and signed by both parties in one of the standard forms. There may be more than one such agreement relating to successive parts of the same project; if so, it is common for them to be in the same standard form. Where there is a formal document such as a JCT form of contract, then it is a mistake to assume that it contains the whole of the contract. It will usually incorporate by reference bills of quantities, drawings and often a specification. These may well contain information pertinent to the dispute. The contract documentation in such a case can often be substantial and it requires some experience to be able quickly to locate the relevant provisions.

Where there is no document signed by both parties, then finding the contract can be extremely difficult and may not be resolved until trial. Frequently one or both parties attempts to incorporate its own standard conditions, its own programme or a particular letter that it may have written. Sometimes the standard conditions contain a clause such as 'The purchaser's order shall be constructed as an express acceptance of these conditions and insofar as any provision of the purchaser's order is inconsistent herewith, these conditions shall be deemed to prevail'. Such a condition is not conclusive (*Butler Machine Tool Co Ltd* v *Ex-Cell-O Corporation (England) Ltd* [1979] 1 All ER 965), and it is necessary to analyse the contract on the traditional basis of offer and acceptance.

In many cases the parties make a series of counter-offers to each other and the acceptance does not occur until one party or the other accepts the last made offer by his conduct in starting work. It is, therefore, particularly important to establish when the works were commenced.

When looking at the formation of the contract, it is helpful to bear in mind the following points

(a) Essential terms

A contract cannot come into being until the essential terms are agreed. It is said in *Keating* that agreement as to parties, price, time and description of works is the minimum necessary, although an

23

obligation to complete within a reasonable time will be implied if the other essential terms are agreed. In the case of contracts other than lump-sum contracts the description of the works may be in extremely broad terms, and even in the case of the lump-sum contracts it is often succinct.

(b) Retrospective agreement

It is apparent from *Trollope and Colls Ltd* v *Atomic Power Constructions Ltd* [1963] 1 WLR 333 that it is perfectly possible for the parties not to form their contract until some time after the work has commenced, such that the terms of the contract operate retrospectively.

(c) Quasi-contract

If there is no agreement as to price then there is no contract, but nonetheless a builder is entitled in quasi-contract to be paid a reasonable sum if he carries out work at the request of the other party.

(d) Incorporation by reference

It is common in the industry for offers to contain such words as 'JCT conditions to apply'. It is perfectly possible for such conditions to be incorporated by reference but conditions such as the JCT conditions are to a large measure meaningless without appointment of an architect or supervising officer, deletion of alternative clauses (such as the clauses which deal with fluctuation) and completion of the appendix which contains such matters as the liquidated damages figure.

(e) Formal requirements

It should be noted that there is no requirement under the Law of Property Act 1925, s 40, for a building contract to be in writing because in normal circumstances the building contract does not dispose of any interest in land. The builder is merely given a licence to enter the land. In the exceptional case of a building lease then it is of course necessary for there to be a signed memorandum under s 40.

(f) Agency

It is a feature of building contracts that negotiations are frequently carried out on behalf of the employer by an agent, often an architect or surveyor. In such cases, the fact of the agency and the identity of the principal are usually disclosed to the contractor. Sometimes, however, the architect or surveyor appears to contract in his own name. In such a case, the contractor can sue either the agent or the principal once the principal's identity is discovered, although the doctrine of election may cause the builder to lose his right to sue one by an unequivocal election to sue the other (*Clarkson Booker* v *Andjel* [1964] 2 QB 775). Usually, either the employer or his agent may sue, although it may be necessary to consider the many cases upon exclusion of undisclosed principals before establishing whether the undisclosed principal may sue in his own name rather than be obliged to sue in the name of his agent.

(g) Unfair Contract Terms Act 1977

Where one or other party puts forward its standard conditions, then substantial parts of those conditions may be written standard terms of business which fail to satisfy the requirement of reasonableness under the terms of the Unfair Contract Terms Act 1977, s 3.

It is submitted in *Keating* (pp 34 and 346) that the JCT form is not to be construed contra proferentem either the employer or the contractor. There has, however, been some speculation as to whether the JCT form might be the 'written standard terms of business' of one or both parties within the meaning of the Unfair Contract Terms Act 1977, s 3(1). It seems unlikely that the draftsman of the Act can have intended to affect the JCT form (if indeed he was even conscious of it), but if the courts were ever to bring the JCT form within the scope of the 1977 Act then it would seem likely that many of the clauses would be affected. In the meantime the courts continue to apply the nineteenth century rules of strict construction to the contract, even where to do so leads to manifest absurdity (*Jarvis* v *Westminster Corporation* [1970] 1 WLR 637 HL).

(h) Liquidated damages clauses

Subject to express agreement, there is normally to be implied into a building contract a term that the contractor will complete the works within a reasonable time. If, without sufficient excuse, the contractor is late in completing the works then he is liable to pay damages at common law assessed under the common law principles that derive from *Hadley* v *Baxendale* (1854) 9 Ex 341 and *Victoria Laundry (Windsor) Ltd* v *Newman Industries Ltd* [1949] 2 KB 528.

Formal building contracts usually quantify precisely both of these common law matters. Not only is the completion date agreed but the amount recoverable by an employer for delay in completion of the works is fixed by a liquidated damages clause. Such a clause appears at Clause 24 of the JCT form of contract.

Unlike the provision at Clause 26 of the JCT contract relating to loss and expense (which deals with the entitlement of the contractor who is delayed by his employer) Clause 24 does not operate to adjust the contract sum, but creates a separate debt due from the contractor to the employer and gives the employer a contractual right of set-off. In other words, the amount of any liquidated damages is not reflected in the amount of the architect's certificates for payment, but is deductible from what would otherwise be payable under those certificates.

There is a distinction in English law between a liquidated damages clause (which is perfectly valid) and a penalty clause (which is unenforceable). Unfortunately, the expression 'penalty clause' is widely used in the industry to mean a liquidated damages clause, and in some other English speaking legal systems the terms are used by lawyers interchangeably. Whether a clause is a penalty clause or a liquidated damages clause depends principally upon its amount; the test was formulated by the House of Lords in *Dunlop Pneumatic Tyre Co Ltd* v *New Garage & Motor Co Ltd* [1915] AC 79 at pp 86-7:

> '1 Though the parties to a contract who use the words 'penalty' or 'liquidated damages' may prima facie be supposed to mean what they say, yet the expression used is not conclusive. The Court must find out whether the payment stipulated is in truth a penalty or liquidated damages . . . .
>
> 2 The essence of a penalty is a payment of money stipulated as *in terrorem* of the offending party; the essence of liquidated damages is a genuine pre-estimate of damage. . . .
>
> 3 The question whether a sum stipulated is a penalty or liquidated damages is a question of construction to be decided upon the terms and inherent circumstances of each particular contract, judged of at the time of the making of the contract, not as at the time of the breach. . . .
>
> 4 To assist this task of construction various tests have been suggested, which if applicable to the case under consideration, may prove helpful, or even conclusive. Such are:
>
> (a) It will be held to be a penalty if the sum stipulated for is extravagant and unconscionable in amount in comparison with the greatest loss which could conceivably be proved to have followed from the breach. . . .
>
> (b) It will be held to be a penalty if the breach consists only in not paying a sum of money, and the sum stipulated is a sum greater than the sum which ought to have been paid. . . .
>
> (c) There is presumption (but no more) that it is a penalty when 'a single lump sum is made payable by way of compensation, on the occurrence of one or more or all of several events, some of which may occasion serious and others but trifling damage'. . . .

On the other hand:

(d) It is no obstacle to the sum stipulated being a genuine pre-estimate of damage, that the consequences of the breach are such as to make precise pre-estimation almost an impossibility. On the contrary, that is just the situation when it is probable that pre-estimated damage was the true bargain between the parties. . . .'

If a clause is found to be a penalty clause, then the employer is entitled to receive by way of damages only that sum which would compensate him for his actual loss, and it seems that the employer may be put to an election as to whether to seek to rely on the clause or not *(Watts, Watts & Co Ltd* v *Mitsui & Co Ltd* [1917] AC 227 HL).

In practice it is comparatively rare to find penalty clauses (in the strict sense of these words) in substantial building contracts. The sum is frequently calculated by reference to interest rates applied to the capital value of the completed works, and it requires only a simple calculation to show that a genuine pre-estimate of the damages that flows from loss of use of a building worth a million pounds can be of the order of £3,000 per week.

2 Implied terms   *

The implication of terms into building contracts is almost entirely a matter of common law; there are no codifying statutes equivalent to the Sale of Goods Acts or the Law of Property Acts. There are some peripheral statutory incursions, such as the Defective Premises Act 1972 (which affects new dwellings outside the NHBC scheme) and the Health and Safety at Work etc Act 1974, s 71 (which, when it comes into effect, will create a statutory cause of action for breach of building regulations), but these statutory provisions do not impinge greatly upon the common law rules.

The absence of a codifying statute leads to a flexibility of approach. Where the parties contract under a lengthy standard form, such as the JCT form, the express provisions will leave little room for substantial implication of terms. On the other hand, where the parties agree the minimum of express terms, then the common law will imply terms that have a familiar ring to those used to sale of goods contracts, such as the fitness for purpose, the quality of the workmanship and materials, and the time for performance.

The more important of the implied terms are considered below, but it is important to note that in building contracts, especially where both parties do or ought to know what they are doing, the courts are often slow to imply terms so as to make the contract reasonable or to iron out the nonsenses and inconsistencies that frequently appear in building contracts. Indeed, one of the leading cases on the limits to implication of terms is a building case, *Trollope & Colls Ltd* v *North West Metropolitan Regional Hospital Board* [1973] 1 WLR 601. In it, the House of Lords said that its function is to interpret and apply the contract which the parties have made for themselves. The court held, in effect, that if the parties contract for a nonsense, then a nonsense they shall have. They said at 609:

> 'If the express terms are perfectly clear and free from ambiguity, there is no choice to be made between different possible meanings: the clear terms must be applied even if the court thinks some other terms would have been more suitable. An unexpressed term can be implied if and only if the court finds that the parties must have intended that term to form part of their contract: it is not enough for the court to find that such a term would have been adopted by the parties as reasonable men if it had been suggested to them: it must have been a term that went without saying, a term *necessary* to give business efficacy to the contract, a term which, though tacit, formed part of the contract which the parties made for themselves.'

The *Trollope & Colls* case represents the House of Lords in a strict constructionist mood. The Court of Appeal has in the past adopted a more adventurous approach (as in *Greaves & Co Contractors* v *Baynham Meikle & Partners* [1975] 1 WLR 1095), and indeed it is clear from the judgments in *Young & Marten Ltd* v *McManus Childs Ltd* [1969] 1 AC 454 that even the House of Lords is prepared to look at policy considerations when considering the implication of terms. In brief, the position seems to be that the terms as to workmanship and materials, fitness for purpose, completion and other matters of principle are now well established and readily implied, whereas the courts are not generally prepared to imply terms to iron out nonsenses arising out of detailed wording in particular contracts.

Unlike the many terms implied by statute in other areas of law, the common law terms implied in building contracts are capable of being ousted by express terms. In *Keating* it is put as follows:

> 'Where there is a comprehensive written contract such as the (JCT) Standard form of building contract there may be very little room for the implication of any terms, for if the parties have dealt expressly with a matter in the contract, no term dealing with the same matter can be implied.'

Those words were written before the impact of the Unfair Contract Terms Act 1977 became apparent, and it still remains to be seen how far that Act will render the implied terms in building contracts as universally applicable as their counterparts in the Sale of Goods Act 1979.

(a) Fitness for purpose   *

A warranty is usually implied on the part of the contractor that the material used in the works and the completed works themselves should be reasonably fit for the purpose for which they are required. There is remarkably little case law supporting this implication since the obligation as to the works as a whole is not generally thought to apply where the contractor is bound to follow a detailed design prepared by the employer's architect. In those circumstances the contractor's obligation is to build what he has been told to build, and it is not his fault if that is ineffective. This term is, however, of particular importance in design-and-build contracts where the contractor's obligation as to the fitness of the completed works is an absolute one, and goes beyond the obligation merely to use reasonable skill and care. (*Keating* points to *Greaves* v *Baynham Meikle* [1975] 1 WLR 1075; *Hudson* points to the reasoning of the House of Lords in *Young & Marten* v *McManus Childs* [1969] 1 AC 454. Now also see *Independent Broadcasting Authority* v *EMI Ltd* (1981) 14 BLR 1.

Ordinarily, it is for the court to determine upon expert evidence whether the works are fit for their purpose in any particular respect. Sometimes, however, the parties pre-agreed what is to be expected of the works in a performance specification. Where, for example, the parties pre-agree the required speed of a lift, the employer will not be able to complain that that speed is not fast enough.

The term for fitness for purpose may be implied in relation to part only of the contract works (*Cammell Laird* v *Manganese Bronze & Brass Co Ltd* [1934] AC 402). This term was also considered, along with *(b)* and *(c)* below, in *Hancock and Others* v *BW Brazier (Anerley) Limited* [1966] 1 WLR 1317 (see *(c)* below for details).

(b) Materials   *

A warranty is usually implied on the part of the contractor that the materials used should be of good quality. This warranty is not overridden by the selection by the employer or the architect of a particular sort of material; in such a case the materials used must be good of their expressed kind.

The extent of this term was considered at length by the House of Lords in *Young & Marten* v *McManus Childs* [1969] 1 AC 454. Particularly difficult questions can arise where the architect nominates a particular supplier or where the materials specified are only obtainable from one manufacturer. It seems from *Young & Marten* v *McManus Childs* that the court will pay particular regard to whether the contractor has any recourse against his sub-contractor or supplier; if so, the court will be more ready to find the contractor liable for any shortcomings in the material, thereby preserving the chain of liability.

This term was also considered, along with *(a)* and *(c)*, in *Hancock v Brazier (Anerley) Limited* [1966] 1 WLR 1317 (see *(c)* below for details).

* *(c) Workmanship*

A warranty is usually implied on the part of the contractor that the work will be carried out in good and workmanlike manner. This term is not affected by any requirement on the contractor to follow a particular design or to use particular materials. By definition, workmanship is that element left to the discretion of the workman.

It may be arguable as a matter of principle that the warranty is excluded where the work is to be carried out to the satisfaction of the employer's architect. In practice, contractors are always held responsible for defects arising out of the bad workmanship of themselves or their sub-contractors, whether nominated or domestic.

This term was considered along with the previous two in relation to a contract for the sale of a house in the course of erection in *Hancock and Others* v *BW Brazier (Anerley) Limited* [1966] 1 WLR 1317. In that case, the sale was made subject to the National Conditions of Sale so far as not inconsistent with the other contract conditions, and Clause 12 of the National Conditions of Sale provided that the purchaser should be deemed to buy with full notice of the actual state of the property and take it as it was. Upon the facts of the case the Court of Appeal rejected Clause 12 of the National Conditions of Sale for repugnance, and found that there was a threefold obligation: to do the work in a good and workmanlike manner, to supply good and proper materials and to provide a house reasonably fit for human habitation. The builder's liability was absolute in the sense of being independent of fault and applied to work done before the contract was entered into as well as subsequent work.

In practice, cases upon the sale of partly completed dwellings will often contain the additional element of a NHBC house purchaser's agreement, and it will then be necessary to consider the terms of that agreement.

(d) Design defects

*   It has been held by the Supreme Court of Canada in *Brunswick Construction* v *Nowlan* ((1975) 49 DLR (3d) 93) that a contractor executing work in accordance with plans of the employer's architect is under a duty to warn the employer of obvious design defects.

There is not any English authority on the point, and both *Hudson* and *Keating* suggest that the case may be wrongly decided.

(e) Indispensably necessary work

Building contracts are usually entire in the sense that the contractor undertakes to complete the work. This imports an obligation not only to do those things particularly described in the contract but also everything else that is indispensably necessary for the completion of the work. In ordinary circumstances a contractor is not entitled to any additional payment for such indispensably necessary work (*Williams* v *Fitzmaurice* (1858) 3 H & N 844).

This obligation may be seen either as a matter of construction of the express terms of the contract or as a matter of implication. In practice, the same result arises upon either analysis.

(f) Progress

Formal building contracts usually include an express provision as to when the contractor must complete the works and also an obligation that the contractor should regularly and diligently proceed with them. Such provision appears in Clause 23.1 of the JCT form.

It is generally agreed that in the absence of such an express provision there is an implied obligation on the contractor to complete the work as a whole in a reasonable time (see *Charnock* v *Liverpool Corporation* [1968] 1 WLR 1498). There is controversy as to whether, in the absence of an express term, there is an implied term as to regular and diligent progress. *Hudson* suggests that there is such an implied term but *Keating* suggests that there is not.

Where a building contract contains an express completion date and the employer does something sufficient to release the contractor from the express completion obligation, then the implied obligation on the contractor to complete within a reasonable time will arise.

(g) By-laws

It is usual for formal contracts to contain an express obligation on the part of the contractor to comply with by-laws and other statutory requirements. Such a clause appears at Clause 6 of the JCT form. In the absence of such an express provision, it is suggested by *Keating* that such a term arises by implication.

In the absence of an express provision, there used to be some doubt as to whether the contractor's obligation to comply with by-laws is absolute or is merely an obligation to exercise care. In *Anns* v *Merton London Borough Council* [1978] AC 728, Lord Wilberforce said:

'. . . since it is the duty of the builder (owner or not) to comply with the byelaws, I would be of opinion that an action could be brought against him in effect, for breach of statutory duty by any person for whose benefit or protection the byelaw was made.'

There is no talk there of any need to show negligence, and it now appears clear from *Eames London Estates Ltd and Others* v *North Hertfordshire District Council and others* (unreported, 31 October 1980, Queen's Bench Division, Official Referee's Business, HH Judge Edgar Fay QC) that the obligation to comply with by-laws is absolute and independent of negligence.

When the Health and Safety at Work Act 1974, s 71, comes into force, then contractors will owe a statutory duty to observe building regulations and other similar by-laws.

(h) Economy in cost contracts

Where there is a cost contract under which the contractor is entitled to be paid the cost of the works, then there is usually an express term requiring the contractor to carry out the works efficiently and not wastefully. If there is not, then it is generally thought that the contractor is not entitled to be paid the costs incurred wastefully or extravagantly.

There is little or no reported case law upon this topic, and although there is general agreement as to the result that the courts would bring about, it is by no means clear whether they would do so as a matter of construction or as a matter of implication of a term.

(i) Possession

It is obvious that the employer must allow the contractor to come onto the site in order to execute the work; the right of the contractor to enter upon the land is generally regarded as a licence (*Hudson* at p 681).

It is suggested in *Hudson* (at p 317) that in the case of a new project the contractor will normally be entitled to exclusive possession of the entire site in the absence of express stipulation to the contrary but that a lesser degree of possession need be afforded in such cases as works of repairs or re-instatement of existing premises while still occupied or in the case of sub-contracts.

Subject to express agreement it is to be implied that the employer should give possession within a reasonable time (*Freeman & Son* v *Hensler* (1900) HBC (4th Ed), Vol 2, p 292).

(j) Instructions

The obligation on the part of the employer to give possession of the site arises as part of an overall implication that he agrees to do all that is necessary on his part to bring about completion of the contract (*MacKay* v *Dick* (1881) 6 App Cas 251). According to the terms of the contract there will generally be other things which the employer must do, such as to supply within a reasonable time particulars of an incomplete design (*Roberts* v *Bury Improvement Commissioners* (1870) LR 5 CP 310); and, if the contract requires one, appoint an architect (*Hunt* v *Bishop* (1853) 8 Ex 675); and, if a nominated sub-contractor goes into liquidation, re-nominate another (*Bickerton & Son Ltd* v *North West Metropolitan Regional Hospital Board* [1969] 1 WLR 607).

(k) Certification

Where the contract provides that an architect or other person has the power to certify as to such matters as interim payment, then the architect must be neutral in that he must act fairly and impartially as between the employer and the contractor. Under the normal forms of contract the architect is not, however, an arbitrator and the power of dismissal rests with the employer. Accordingly, if to the employer's knowledge the architect persists in applying the contract rules wrongly in his capacity as certifier, then the employer will be in breach of an implied term if he does not dismiss the architect and appoint another (*Panamena Europea Navigacion* v *Frederick Leyland & Co Ltd* [1947] AC 428).

There is, however, another view of the *Panamena* case; namely, that its effect is not to impose a positive obligation on the employer to replace the certifier in the circumstances, but that failure to do so releases the contractor from the necessity to obtain certification before recovering money due.

In practice it is extremely rare for an employer to dismiss an architect in consequence of the architect's bias towards the employer; the point is usually of academic interest by the time any dispute comes to trial, but for tactical reasons contractors sometimes demand that the employer dismiss the architect for failure to issue proper certificates when due.

(l) Interim payment

There is surprisingly little modern case law upon a contractor's implied right to interim payment.

Most building contracts are entire contracts in the sense that the contractor's right to payment is conditional upon his substantial completion of the works. It is a corollary of this as a matter of law that the contractor has no implied right to interim payment. There are, however, some old cases which suggest that there is an implied term for interim payment in contracts for the execution of substantial work. In *The Tergeste* [1903] 87 LT 567 it was said:

'The law follows good sense and business as shown by the case of *Roberts* v *Havelock*. A man who contracts to do a long costly piece of work, does not contract, unless he says so, that he will do all the work, standing out of pocket until he is paid at the end ... and if ... payment is not made, then the shipwright or other artificer is entitled to review his work, and say; "I have done work worth so much, true I have contracted to do other work but it is not reasonable that I should do it, as I have not been paid; and in respect of work that I have done I claim payment".'

In practical terms, the courts are quick to find a provision for interim payment as a matter of construction, and the use of such vague expressions as 'terms monthly' will probably be sufficient for the court to find an agreement for interim payment.

There is a practical importance of whether there is an implied term, if none is expressed, for interim payment as regards repudiation. If a contractor is not being paid and has in mind to abandon the works then either the contractor or the employer will have been in breach according to whether there is a term calling for interim payment. In either case the contractor will be entitled to payment or credit for the work he has done but the result as regards the contractor's loss of profit and the employer's loss of bargain in respect of the remaining work is usually very different.

(m) Final payment

Where a contractor does work for and at the request of an employer, and there is no express agreement as to price, then the law implies an obligation on the employer to pay the contractor a reasonable sum for the contractor's labour and materials supplied (*Moffatt* v *Laurie* (1855) 15 CB 583). It is usually immaterial in practice whether, upon a true analysis, the obligation arises in contract or in quasi-contract.

Likewise, where an employer orders extra work, then he impliedly, if not expressly, agrees to pay for it. Where such extra work is of the kind contemplated by the contract and there are contract rates for it, then the employer must pay at the contract rate. Where there are no contract rates or the work is outside the scope of the original contract, then the employer must pay a reasonable sum (*Thorn* v *London Corporation* (1876) 1 App Cas 120).

There are no universally applicable rules used by the courts in determining what is a reasonable sum. Sometimes the court takes the actual cost of the works to the contractor and adds a reasonable percentage for profit; sometimes it takes expert evidence upon what an employer could reasonably expect to have to pay for the sort of work in question.

Chapter 4

Payment under Lump-sum Contracts

1 Adjustments to the lump sum

Where the consideration for a building contract is a pre-agreed lump sum, then that lump sum is prima facie the sum which the contractor is ultimately entitled to at the end of the day. It is, however, usually the case that the lump sum will be subject to adjustment in respect of such matters as variations, fluctuations, prime-cost sum, provisional sums, and loss and expense. If the contract is described as 'fixed price' this merely means that the lump sum is not to be adjusted in respect of fluctuations; it remains liable to be adjusted in respect of the other matters.

There follows a brief description of the more important of these adjustments. There are others which sometimes fall to be made; the adjustment clause in the JCT contract, Clause 30.6.2, provides sixteen separate heads of adjustment.

(a) Variations

In most standard form building contracts there is a provision expressly entitling the architect to issue instructions requiring a variation from the works originally contracted for. Such a provision appears at Clause 13.2 of the JCT contract. Such a variation may be for the addition, omission or substitution of any of the original work, although in practice many variations amount to the ordering of extras. In informal contracts the employer may simply change his mind as to the work he requires.

In either case, the contractor is entitled to be paid for extra work. In the JCT contract there are rules at Clause 13.5 as to the rate of payment in respect of variations.

Where there is no express agreement as to the rate of payment for extra work but the lump sum is calculated by reference to contract rates, then there may be an implication that extra work of the same kind should be paid for at the same rates. If not then the employer must pay a reasonable sum in respect of varied works (*Sir Lindsay Parkinson & Co Ltd* v *Commissioners of His Majesty's Works and Public Buildings* [1949] 2 KB 632).

It is traditional for the effect of variations in the works upon the lump sum to be set out in the form of a bill of variations. A bill of variations is usually set out as an account that starts with the contract sum, deducts by way of omission any item which has been varied and adds back the total price of such items as varied.

(b) Fluctuations

Inflation in the construction industry is as much a fact of modern life as elsewhere. Contractors frequently have to estimate the cost of work many months or even sometimes years before that work is to be performed. They often also work to comparatively small profit margins, and they therefore frequently protect themselves against the effect of increases of cost of both labour and materials by inserting an express provision in the contract for the lump sum to be adjusted to reflect changes in the cost of taxes, labour and materials. Where such clauses envisage only rises in costs they are often called 'increased-cost clauses'. Where they also envisage the (perhaps remote) possibility of decreases in cost, then they are generally known as 'fluctuation clauses'.

Fluctuation clauses can take many forms. The fluctuations clause in the present JCT form of contract contains complex alternatives and runs to some 7,500 words. At the other end of the scale, small builders often insert the simplest clauses in their standard conditions entitling them to pass on increased costs to the employer.

Fluctuation clauses are not generally regarded as unreasonable provisions entitling contractors to extra money upon demand. Indeed, it is commonly found that the complex provisions in the JCT form of contract allow a contractor to recover only about 60% of the true cost to him of any increases in cost that occur after the date of the tender. A properly worded fluctuation clause represents an entirely reasonable agreement to share the risk of inflation.

The expression 'fixed-price contract' is used to denote a contract which does not contain a fluctuations or an increased costs clause. The expression does *not* mean that the price is fixed for all other purposes, and indeed the lump sum will frequently be subject to adjustment in respect to such matters as variations.

For a brief description of the fluctuations clauses in the JCT form of contract, see p 9.

(c) Prime-costs sums

Where the employer nominates a sub-contractor, the entitlement of the contractor in respect of such sub-contracted work is usually what the contractor must pay the sub-contractor plus a 2½% main contractor's discount. The amount the contractor must pay the sub-contractor is usually not known until after completion of the sub-contract work, and it is traditional for the employer's architect or quantity surveyor to include a prime-cost sum in the bills of quantities. This is, in effect, the architect or quantity surveyor's pre-estimate of what the nominated sub-contractor's final account will eventually be, and at the conclusion of the main contract the prime-cost sum is deducted and there is substituted the amount finally payable to the nominated sub-contractor.

In the JCT form of contract these adjustments appear at Clause 30.6.2.1 and 30.6.2.7.

(d) Provisional sums

It sometimes happens that at the time of the formation of the contract the employer or his architect has yet to decide upon the precise extent of a part of the work but does anticipate that some work in that area will be necessary. It is of course possible for such work to be ignored altogether in the bills of quantities and for the work to be subsequently ordered as extra work. Alternatively, the architect or quantity surveyor may include a provisional sum in the bills of quantities, and such a provisional sum is the architect's or quantity surveyor's approximate estimate of the value of the work which will in due course be ordered. The architect then must during the course of the work issue an instruction to the contractor as to what work is required in that area, and if he decides to have the work performed by a nominated sub-contractor he is usually entitled to do so.

Where there is a provisional sum, the contract sum is adjusted by omitting the provisional sum and adding back the actual price of the work ordered. In the JCT form of contract such work is valued in the same way as variations under Clause 13, and the adjustment to the contract sum falls to be made under Clause 30.6.2.13.

(e) Loss and expense

Many contracts reserve to the employer or his architect a wide-ranging right to issue instructions to the contractor. These instructions can frequently cause the contractor extra expense that is not necessarily reflected in any additional payment he receives for any variation of the work itself. Likewise, delay by the employer's architect in providing the contractor with necessary details of the design of the works is likely to cause delay to the contractor. Similarly, other acts or defaults of the employer or his architect, such as failure to give prompt possession of the site or unnecessary requirements for the opening up for the inspection of work, can cause loss to the contractor. For these reasons it is common to insert a provision in building contracts that in such circumstances the contractor is entitled to an addition to the contract sum, and this addition is usually described as 'loss and expense'.

Frequently, a provision for loss and expense merely means that the contractor is entitled to be paid in respect of some matter *under* the contract rather than by way of damages for *breach* of contract. Sophisticated arguments can arise as to whether such a matter gives rise to a claim for loss and expense by the contractor under the contract or a claim for damages for breach of contract. The argument is usually sterile since the measure of compensation for the contractor is the same in either case; see p 42 and *Wraight Ltd* v *PH & T (Holdings) Ltd* (1968) 13 BLR 26.

Loss and expense frequently arises where the works are delayed for some reason. Sub-contractors are often involved and a complex web of claims, and cross-claims can occur; see below.

In the JCT form of contract the loss and expense clause appears at Clause 26 and the appropriate adjustment to the contract sum falls to be made under Clause 30.6.2.14.

2 Delay, prolongation and disruption

Things can and do go wrong in building contracts. The ordering of extra work can disrupt progress, the architect can be late in producing drawings, the contractor can be slow in getting on with the work, one of the nominated or domestic sub-contractors can delay things, or the works might be disrupted by some entirely neutral cause (like exceptionally adverse weather conditions). All these matters can cause substantial financial losses to the parties involved, and there follows a review of the basic consequences of these matters in the case of a lump-sum contract where the JCT form has been used.

(a) Extra work

Where the employer orders extra works, then he must pay for them. If the extra works disturb or delay the contract as a whole, the contractor is entitled to loss and expense under Clause 26.2.7. Where the extra works affect the regular progress of a nominated sub-contractor (whether or not it is the sub-contractor himself who is required to execute the extra work), then the nominated sub-contractor is also entitled to loss and expense (Clause 13.1.2.7 of NSC/4).

The position of a domestic sub-contractor depends upon the terms of the contract between the main contractor and the domestic sub-contractor. Under the Blue Form the sub-contractor's entitlement to payment for varied work is set out in Clause 12 (2); the provision in Clause 10 (1) that the contractor shall make available to the sub-contractor the benefit of any right under the main contract is difficult to construe and is probably meaningless. If the regular progress of the domestic sub-contractor's work is disturbed by extra work executed by the contractor or by another sub-contractor, then the domestic sub-contractor may be entitled to damages at common law against the main contractor.

If the extra works cause a delay in the completion of the works as a whole, then the contractor is entitled to an extension of time under Clause 25.4.5.1 of the main contract. Nominated sub-contractors get an extension of time under Clause 11.2.5.5.1 of NSC/4. Domestic sub-contractors get an extension under Clause 9 (3) (a) of the Blue Form.

(b) Employer default

It is not uncommon for contracts to be delayed by reason of the architect, who is the agent of the employer, being late in providing necessary instructions, drawings, details or levels to the contractor. If such delay disrupts the regular progress of the works, then the contractor is entitled to be paid loss and expense (Clause 26.2.1). The same result flows from a number of other matters listed in Clause 26.2, and the position is much the same as in the case of extra work. Nominated sub-contractors may be entitled to loss and expense under Clause 13.1 of NSC/4 and domestic sub-contractors may have a claim for damages against the main contractor at common law.

The main contractor gets an extension of time under Clause 25. Nominated sub-contractors get an extension of time under Clause 11 of NSC/4 and domestic sub-contractors on the Blue Form get an extension of time under Clause 9 (1) (a).

(c) Contractor default

The main contractor sometimes fails to complete the work by the completion date and has no one but himself to blame. If so, the architect must issue a certificate to that effect (Clause 24.1); and if the employer so requires, the contractor must pay or allow liquidated damages at the rate stated in the appendix to the contract (Clause 24.2.1). In other words, the contractor must compensate the employer for the employer's loss arising out of the delay, and of course the contractor has no claim against the employer for his own additional costs arising out of his own delay.

The terminology under the 1980 edition of the JCT form is confusing, and the completion date must be distinguished from the date for completion. The date for completion is the date that appears in the appendix to the contract and prima facie this is the date by which the contractor must finish the works. The completion date, on the other hand, can be altered and broadly means that the date for completion as extended (Clause 1.3). Accordingly, the obligation on the contractor to complete the works by the completion date represents an obligation on the contractor to complete by the date for completion as extended. Any matter which entitles the contractor to an extension is called a 'relevant event' (Clause 25). If the contractor's defaults affect the regular progress of the work of the nominated sub-contractor then the sub-contractor gets an extension of time as against the main contractor (Clause 11.2.2.1 of NSC/4). That extension of time is dealt with by the written consent of the architect. The sub-contractor is further entitled to be paid loss and expense (or perhaps damages) by the main contractor but this is not dealt with through the certification process. If the amount of such loss and expense can be agreed between the contractor and the sub-contractor, then Clause 13.2 of NSC/4 applies; if agreement is not possible then either a reasonable amount is due under the sub-contract or the sub-contractor may be entitled to damages at common law.

The position of the domestic sub-contractor is much the same as the nominated sub-contractor, except that the architect is not involved in the sub-contractor's entitlement to an extension of time. A provision similar to Clause 13.2 of NSC/4 appears at Clause 10 (2) of the Blue Form.

(d) Nominated sub-contractor default

Where a nominated sub-contractor delays completion of the whole works, complex provisions come into play, the effect of which is that the sub-contractor must pay the losses of every affected party.

Under the main contract, the contractor is entitled to an extension of time from the employer (Clause 25.4.7) but is not entitled as against the employer to loss and expense. The employer, therefore, does not recover his losses from the contractor. The employer may, however, have a claim against the nominated sub-contractor directly under Clause 3.4 of NSC/2 (in which the nominated sub-contractor warrants to the employer directly that the contractor will not become entitled to any extension of time under Clause 25.4.7). It is not clear from NSC/2 whether the amount of damages payable by a nominated sub-contractor under this provision is supposed to be liquidated at the rate of liquidated damages in the main contract.

Under the nominated sub-contract NSC/4 the sub-contractor is liable to the main contractor for any loss or damage suffered or incurred by the contractor and caused by the failure of the nominated sub-contractor to complete on time (Clause 12.2 of NSC/4). There is a proviso, however, that the contractor is not entitled to claim such loss or damage unless the architect is issued an appropriate certificate under Clause 35.15 of the main contract. Certificates under Clause 35.15 of the main contract will probably continue for some years to be known by the clause numbering in the 1963 edition— Clause 27 (d) (ii). Interestingly, this proviso only applies where the sub-contractor delays and not where the sub-contractor disrupts the main contractor's progress without delaying completion (Clause 13.3 of NSC/4).

The amount of the main contractor's claim against the nominated sub-contractor does not, of course, generally include the employer's losses (which are recovered by the employer directly from the nominated sub-contractor under Clause 3.4 of NSC/2) and this is an exception to the normal rule that liability flows 'up the line'.

(e) Domestic sub-contractor default

Where the works are delayed by the default of the domestic sub-contractor, the end result is much the same as in the case of default by a nominated sub-contractor but the mechanism is different.

Under the main contract, the contractor is not entitled to any extension of time, and it is as though the defaults of the domestic sub-contractor were the defaults of the main contractor himself. The main contractor must therefore pay liquidated damages to the employer in respect of such delay as is caused by domestic sub-contractors.

Under the sub-contract, the domestic sub-contractor will usually be liable to the main contractor in damages at common law not only for the main contractor's own losses but also for what liquidated damages the main contractor must pay or allow to the employer. Where the sub-contract is in the Blue Form, then the contractor may have an alternative claim under the contract under Clause 10 (3) and certain rules as to set-off appear at Clause 15 (2); there is however no requirement on the contractor to obtain any architect's certificate before making a claim.

Ordinarily of course there is no direct contractual nexus between an employer and a domestic sub-contractor, and hence nothing analogous to Clause 3.4 of NSC/2.

(f) Neutral causes

Sometimes the works are disrupted or delayed by matters such as exceptionally adverse weather conditions or strikes, which are beyond the control of any of the parties. In these circumstances the effect of the rule is generally that the losses lie where they fall.

The main contractor is entitled to an extension of time under Clause 25, and therefore does not have to pay the employer liquidated damages in respect of delay occasioned by neutral causes. There is no right for the contractor to be paid loss and expense following the occurrence of neutral causes, and a similar position arises in the standard sub-contract forms applicable to both nominated sub-contractors (NSC/4) and domestic sub-contractors (the Blue Form).

(g) The quantification of loss and expense

The principles applicable to the quantification of loss and expense pursuant to the terms of a building contract are the same as the principles for the assessment of damages for breach of contract (*Wraight Ltd* v *PH & T (Holdings) Ltd* (1968) 13 BLR 26). The context of the calculation is, however, firmly that of the construction industry, and proper quantification of loss and expense in a complex case requires both the knowledge and experience of professional quantity surveyors and the application of legal principles by lawyers.

There are two main heads of loss and expense that usually accompany delay. Firstly, the contractor will have to maintain on site those things that are exclusively referable to the particular contract. Examples of such things are the cost of the site office, site supervision, scaffolding, plant, canteen and so on. The proper re-imbursement under this head is the actual cost of these things to the contractor during the period of delay. It is a matter of arithmetic. Sometimes, contractors prepare a claim on the basis of 'extended preliminaries', where they extrapolate the rates in the preliminaries bill in the bills of quantities; that is sometimes thought among specialist practitioners to be wrong in principle. In *Wraight Ltd* v *PH & T (Holdings) Ltd* Megaw J said: 'In my judgment, there are no grounds for giving to the words "direct loss and/or damage caused to the Contractor by the determination" any other meaning than that which they have, for example, in a case of breach of contract or other question of the relationship of a fault to damage in a legal context.'

That judgment related to a determination clause, but it is thought that there is no difference in principle in the case of a loss and expense clause; loss and expense is quantified in the same way as damages at common law, and that means the actual cost to the contractor; see *Hadley* v *Baxendale* (1854) 9 Ex 341 and *Victoria Laundry (Windsor) Ltd* v *Newman Industries/Coulson & Co* [1949] 2 KB 528.

There is also another head, that of Head Office overheads (also known as off-site costs) and profit. These two are sometimes known as gross profit, and the contractor is entitled to be compensated in respect of them (*Wraight Ltd* v *PH & T Holdings Ltd* (1968) 13

BLR 26). The calculation of loss and expense in this area is far more difficult than for the on-site costs, since head office overheads and profit cannot usually be seen as exclusively referable to any particular contract. It is necessary to adopt some sort of formula method.

The formula most commonly used is the 'Hudson Formula', which appears in *Hudson* at p 599. It says that a contractor's loss and expense in terms of head office overheads and profit resulting from delay is:

$$\frac{\text{HO/Profit Percentage}}{100} \times \frac{\text{Contract Sum}}{\text{Contract Period}} \times \text{Period of Delay}$$

The effect of the formula is to calculate the rate at which the contractor would have earned gross profit had the contract run to time and to extrapolate that rate into the period of delay.

The Hudson formula is of vital importance in loss and expense cases. Quantity surveyors frequently fail to understand it, and contractors who ignore it often pass up a large proportion of their total entitlement. However, it raises difficult issues as to the measure of damages at common law and all too often it is beyond the professional experience of both the general practitioner lawyer and the quantity surveyor.

There is another issue of considerable importance in the quantification of loss and expense: that of financing charges. Building contract litigation can take a long time and there is much difference between simple interest at the judgment rate and compound interest at a commercial rate. Take, for example, a loss of £10,000 incurred five years ago. Simple interest at the current judgment rate, 12½%, would be £6,250. Compound interest at 18% with quarterly rests would be £13,078.

It is because of this major factor that attention has recently focused upon the possibility of claiming financing charges as loss and expense rather than interest under the Law Reform (Miscellaneous Provisions) Act 1934. The principle of this was vindicated by the Court of Appeal in *FG Minter Ltd* v *Welsh Health Technical Services Organisation* (1980) 13 BLR 1. Stephenson LJ said:

'I do not think that today we should allow medieval abhorrence to usury to make us shrink from implying a promise to pay interest in a contract if by refusing to imply it we thereby deprive a party of what the contract appears on its natural interpretation to give him . . . .

'In the context of this building contract and the accepted "cash flow" procedure and practice I have no doubt that the two kinds of interest claimed here are direct loss and/or expense unless there is something in the contractual machinery for paying direct loss and/or expense which excludes this loss and expense of interest by the Claimants.'

In principle, therefore, financing charges are recoverable, although the period for which they are recoverable will depend upon the precise wording of the contract. Where the JCT Standard Contract 1963 edition is in issue, it may be that a contractor can only recover financing charges for the whole of the relevant period if he seeks damages at common law from the employer for breach of the employer's implied obligation to ensure that the architect certifies in accordance with his mandate and within a reasonable time (see *Perini Corporation* v *Commonwealth of Australia* (Supreme Court of New South Wales) (1969) 12 BLR 82).

Chapter 5
Preliminary Considerations

There are those who consider litigation as being a last resort. If they are unable to achieve their desired results by commercial means they pass their papers to a litigation solicitor and expect that the next step (apart from some merely procedural matters) will be trial. In building contract matters, that attitude is generally a disastrous mistake. It can lead to vast unnecessary cost, delay, and lost opportunity.

The principal and distinguishing feature of building contracts litigation is the multiplicity of issues to which it gives rise. Very commonly, the failure of the parties to resolve one issue upon a commercial basis does not mean that there is no prospect of resolving other issues upon a commercial basis. There are frequently several parties involved, some of whom may be involved in the litigation and some of whom may not be. The issue of a writ or the service of an arbitration notice should not shock the parties into inaction.

What follows is not intended to be a comprehensive check list. Every case is different. It is, however, intended to indicate the sort of points which merit consideration at an early stage when the prospect of litigation first emerges.

1 Claim by employer for defects

The legal consequences of defects in work are extremely diverse. The observations that follow concern matters of general importance and are in no particular order. (As to who to sue, see p 64.)

(a) Notices

When a defect in building work occurs it is almost always desirable to give notice of the fact to every party that is or may be responsible for it. There are at least three reasons for this.

(i) The responsible party may be willing to do something about the defect at his own cost, particularly where the responsible party is a contractor or sub-contractor. Some contracts, such as the JCT standard form, contain express provision that the contractor should not only be obliged but is also entitled to remedy defects appearing

45

within the defects liability period. As a matter of common law, an employer who fails to give a contractor an opportunity to make good his defects without good cause is in breach of his duty to mitigate his loss; in practice, good cause usually means performance by the contractor so abysmal that the employer could not reasonably be expected to allow the contractor back on site. Many employers are reluctant to allow contractors back to remedy works. They should, however, reflect very carefully before turning down any offer by a contractor to rectify defects without cost.

(ii) Identifying the cause of a defect is often more difficult than it seems. A defect that appears to be a defect of workmanship attributable to a contractor frequently turns out, upon listening to the contractor's account, to be wholly or partly a design matter, the responsibility of the architect. The sooner an employer can form an accurate view as to responsibility the better, and putting a party on notice of a defect implies an invitation to that party to put forward his own account of the cause of the defects.

(iii) Queen's Bench Masters are pragmatists. Time and again, they have seen employers attempting to evade payment of their debt by putting forward trumped-up counter-claims as to defects. On the whole, the later a claim for defects is made, the more likely it is to be regarded as a mere excuse for non-payment. For this reason, where the contractor has a claim for payment, the sooner the employer makes a complaint of the defect the better chance the employer has of resisting an application by the contractor for summary judgment.

The list of potential claimees is a lengthy one. The employer should consider the potential liability not only of the contractor but also of any sub-contractor (under a direct warranty agreement or in negligence), architect, surveyor, engineer, local authority, bondsman or the NHBC. See p 64.

Where the employer suspects that there are defects in the works under a JCT contract, then he should urgently consider the position if the architect issues a final certificate because this is expressed to represent conclusive evidence as to the quality of materials and standard of workmanship unless arbitration or other proceedings are commenced within fourteen days after the final certificate has been issued (Clause 30.9).

(b) Leases

Sometimes the employer is either the landlord or the tenant under a lease. If so it is necessary to look at the lease to see whether it is the landlord or the tenant who is responsible inter se for the defects. That party is not always the same as the building employer, and the loss caused by the defects may not be that of the building employer.

In these circumstances it can be very useful for the landlord and the tenant to cooperate from the outset and arrangements are sometimes made for one to take the other's name in litigation or for the landlord and the tenant to sue as joint plaintiffs, one giving the other an indemnity as to costs.

(c) Formal contracts

Where there is a formal contract (eg the JCT standard form), then there are special considerations that arise.

Formal contracts almost always vest powers in the architect concerning defects. Usually, the architect has powers exercisable during the execution of the work to require the contractor to remedy defective work and to open up for inspection any suspect work. If the architect fails to exercise these powers, then it is often useful for the employer to invite him to do so in writing.

Formal contracts also generally contain determination clauses that entitle either party to terminate the contract upon certain specified breaches and usually subject to service of notices. No general guidance can be given as to the desirability of operating such a clause, save that the decision is frequently difficult and that if it is decided to determine every care should be taken to ensure that the procedures in the clause are precisely followed. It is widely said that the wrongful purported use of a determination clause is itself a repudiatory breach of contract, which gives rise to liability in damages.

The scheme of the JCT contract is that the architect should not issue a *final* certificate until the contractor has remedied all defects. If, however, the architect is on the point of issuing a final certificate notwithstanding the possibility of defects, then the employer is well advised to consider the protection of issuing a generally endorsed writ and serving an arbitration notice. If he fails to do so, the final certificate may be fatal to his claim.

Where the contractor is in delay in achieving completion of the works, the employer may be entitled to deduct liquidated damages. The old procedure in the 1963 edition of the JCT contract has been altered in the 1980 form of contract; in each case it is necessary for the architect and the employer to have careful regard to the necessary notices required.

(d) Repudiation

Even where there is no formal contract, a contractor's workmanship may be of such an appalling standard that the employer is entitled to regard the contract as repudiated and to order the contractor from the site.

Repudiation is a common law right, and because of the generally cumulative nature of building defects sufficiently severe to amount to repudiation, it is important that the right be exercised clearly and decisively, without half measures.

If during the course of an informal building contract the contractor appears to be doing everything wrong during the course of the works, then it is usually best if the employer wishes to repudiate first of all to require the contractor to remedy all the accumulated defects within, say, seven days. If the contractor fails to comply with this requirement, then the notice of repudiation should be written promptly and unequivocally, containing such words as:

> These defects and your failure to remedy them, represent a repudiatory breach of contract, which our client accepts as such. You are required to vacate the site immediately, and in due course a claim will be made against you for the losses suffered by our client.

In the case of a lump-sum contract, where there is no right for the contractor to be paid in instalments, a failure on the part of the contractor to achieve substantial completion disentitles the contractor to any payment at all, see p 1. This can be a factor in deciding when, if at all, to accept appalling workmanship as repudiatory breach. If the repudiation is accepted early enough then the employer may not have to pay anything to the contractor. If the repudiation is left too late it may be difficult to persuade the court that the contractor should receive nothing for his work done, and the employer would have to pay the agreed price less a proper set-off for defects and omissions.

(e) NHBC

The procedure for making a claim under the National House Builders Council rules is apparent from the House Purchasers Agreement and the claim form. It is, however, worth bearing in mind the restrictive meaning given to the word 'structure' in the House Purchasers Agreement and it seems clear from *County & District Properties* v *C Jenner & Son Ltd* [1976] 2 Lloyd's Rep 728 that an employer or house owner is entitled to the contractor for declaratory relief before or at the same time as making a claim against the NHBC notwithstanding clause 8(b) of the House Purchasers Agreement, which reads as follows:

> 'Nothing in this Clause shall be construed as relieving the Vendor of any of his obligations to the Purchaser howsoever they may arise provided that the Purchaser shall before pursuing any claim against the Vendor on account of any defect in the dwelling appearing after the Initial Guarantee Period in respect of which he may by virtue of this Clause have any claim against the Council first pursue his remedy against the Council and any relief obtained from the Council shall be taken into account in mitigation of damages against the Vendor.'

There is usually little point in making such a claim prematurely unless there is a limitation danger. If there is a limitation danger which renders it desirable to bring protective proceedings against the contractor, the costs position will be improved if the contractor has declined a written invitation prior to the issue of proceedings to accept responsibility for the defects if and to the extent that the NHBC fails to do so.

The address of the NHBC is Chiltern Avenue, Amersham, Bucks HP6 5AP (Tel Amersham 4477).

(f) Inspection

Employers sometimes overlook the desirability of contractors and their advisers being offered the opportunity to inspect defects. Without inspection, a contractor may not have any details of latent defects. Defects frequently appear only after the contractor has left the site, and it is entirely reasonable that not only the contractor but also his advisers and experts should be permitted to inspect the defects (and, where appropriate, take photographs, measurements and samples).

The court has power to order such steps under Ord 16 of the Rules of the Supreme Court and a similar power is to be found in the Arbitration Act 1950 in relation to arbitration proceedings. An unreasonable refusal by an employer to offer or allow inspection is bound to influence a court or an arbitrator against the employer. Where a claim has been made against an architect or some other person not being the contractor, the need to offer inspection is of even more importance.

The courts generally recognise the importance of remedying building works, and it is rarely necessary for an employer to delay necessary remedial work merely because of inspection. Seven days' notice to inspect may be entirely sufficient, and if a contractor or his advisers cannot re-arrange their diaries so as to inspect before remedial works commence, then they have no one but themselves to blame.

Is it necessary for the lawyers to inspect the locus in quo? In practice, it is surprisingly rare for such an inspection to be of great value. It can, however, be very useful to enable the lawyers to understand the geography of the site, not only where the site is a large building or complex of buildings but also where it is a small semi-detached house. Without a view, expressions like 'the main area flat roof' and 'the dining room' can be difficult to relate to expressions like 'the production hall roof' or 'the front room'.

As regards defects themselves, lawyers inspecting the site must beware of drawing their own conclusions. What looks to the layman like surface cracking can be symptomatic of major structural damage and an area that looks like a bomb site may require only clearing away. In many cases, a good annotated plan is far more useful to the lawyers than a site inspection.

(g) Photographs

Photographs may be admissible in evidence in litigation and in arbitration. Whoever takes photographs should make a contemporaneous record setting out precisely when and where each photograph is taken, together with if possible a written description of what is being photographed.

It is sometimes worth bearing in mind that film is very cheap, and it may be worthwhile taking many photographs which may or may not subsequently merit the expense of developing.

(h) Immediate settlement

In a formal building contract there are elaborate provisions as to payment of the contractor and the remedying of defects during the execution of the works and during the defects liability period. In the case of informal contracts, however, it is sometimes tempting for an employer to seek an immediate resolution of the issue of defects by agreeing a reduction with the contractor of the contractor's account in respect of the shortcomings in the works. Where there is a possibility that there may be further defects in the works, then this is a dangerous course for the employer to take since he may have compromised the whole of his rights of action against the contractor (*Conquer* v *Boot* [1928] 2 KB 336). It seems that what is settled is not the rights in respect of the *defect* in question (eg the leaking roof) but the *breach* (eg the breach of the obligation to do the work in a good and workmanlike manner). If the employer wishes a settlement at the outset, he must therefore limit the terms of that settlement to the particular defects that he has in mind.

Arbitration is sometimes seen as a species of settlement. This may be so in theory but in practice arbitrators are required to adhere as closely as possible to the procedure in courts of law, and in the ordinary course of events arbitration is no short cut. There are, however, two devices that are sometimes used:

(a) It is sometimes possible and desirable to agree a simplified arbitration process, whereby a pre-agreed arbitrator makes a single inspection to the site and makes an immediate award without any pleadings or other representation, or discovery, or trial. This device can be useful where both parties have a genuine desire to resolve a dispute about a straightforward matter and to abide by the decision of a mutually-agreed arbitrator. Where there is not that mutual desire, the procedure can be a recipe for disaster and leads only to further complication of the issues.

(b) Where there are defects about which there is a dispute as to responsibility but which require prompt remedying, there may be scope for a without prejudice funding arrangement, see p 162

(i) Limitation

Allowing a limitation period to expire without taking protective steps is often understandable but usually inexcusable. A fuller discussion of limitation issues appears at page 158.

At this point it should be noted that limitation often operates as a gradual erosion rather than as a sudden event and the date to note in a diary for the issue of a writ *and* service of an arbitration notice (if there is an arbitration clause) is six years from the date when the employer first discussed the works with his architect and/or contractor, and/or sub-contractors since that is when he can begin to lose any rights in misrepresentation and collateral warranty.

(j) Remedial work

Where an employer has a claim in respect of defects where remedial work is necessary, it is almost always best if he can have had executed and paid for these works before trial. Courts tend to be conservative about estimates of building cost and the best possible evidence of the cost of remedial work is to have spent it. Accordingly, if an employer can afford remedial works it is usually best from a legal point of view for him to do so.

2 Claim by contractor for payment

In their simplest form, claims by contractors for payment are debts, recoverable under Ord 14. It is in the employer's interest to introduce complications to deprive the claim of its quality as a debt; it is in the contractor's interest to present his claim as simply as possible, and as like to a debt as possible. See p 102.

The basic procedure on behalf of a contractor claiming payment is, therefore, to write a seven-day letter, followed by a writ in as uncomplicated a form as possible, followed by an Ord 14 summons.

(a) Non-certification

Where there is a formal contract containing a provision for certification of sums due, the contractor is in difficulties without the necessary certificate or certificates for payment.

It is often the case that architects issue certificates where there is no formal contract empowering them to do so. In those circumstances the contractor does not need a certificate and can simply sue for the price of his work.

Where there is a contract that plainly envisages certification, then the contractor should obtain proper certification from the architect if he can. If the architect is showing bias in favour of the employer, then it is entirely proper to write to him pointing out that he is in breach of his duty to act fairly and impartially between the parties, and potentially liable to the contractor in damages (*Sutcliffe* v *Thackrah* [1974] AC 727). It further appears from *Panamena Europa Navigacion* v *Frederick Leyland & Co Ltd* [1947] AC 428 that the employer should dismiss the architect in such circumstances and from *Perini Corporation* v *Commonwealth of Australia* (1969) 12 BLR 82 that the employer may be liable in damages for the failure of his architect to certify properly. A letter to the employer pointing out these cases sometimes has a beneficial effect.

If the architect is not showing bias in the employer's favour, a different tactical position arises. The architect should be persuaded into issuing the appropriate certificate and assisted in the task of explaining the position to the employer. If the architect persists in his refusal properly to certify payment, then there may be no alternative but to serve an arbitration notice and/or issue proceedings, which are each generally thought to each have the effect of rendering the architect *functus officio* in respect of the matters in dispute. The absence of certification may prevent the contractor from recovering under Ord 14 or resisting a section 4 summons but at trial the state of interim certification is generally regarded as irrelevant to the contractor's entitlement.

(b) Notice

Under most formal contracts it is necessary for the contractor to give notice of various matters before becoming entitled to extensions of time and loss and expense. The importance of these notices in the ICE form of contract was recognised in *Crosby* v *Portland UDC* (1967) 5 BLR 121 and any steps that can be taken to give notices where necessary should be taken.

Where the architect issues a final certificate under the JCT contract, then the parties have fourteen days from the issue of that certificate to commence arbitration or other proceedings (Clause 30.9.3). If proceedings are not commenced within that time the final certificate is expressed to represent conclusive evidence as to various matters connected with payment.

(c) Determination and repudiation

In the case of a formal contract there will generally be a provision entitling the contractor to determine the contract if the employer fails to honour certificates. Provisions in such clauses as to notices must be closely adhered to. A comparable right exists at common law in informal contracts where there is a right to interim payment but not otherwise. See p 33.

In practice, the courts tend to hesitate before giving Ord 14 judgment on a determination or repudiation claim. The court often sees such cases as 'six of one and half a dozen of the other'. It is, therefore, usually desirable from a contractor's point of view not to determine or accept a repudiation towards the end of building works but to complete them and then sue for the price in the ordinary way.

(d) Defects and set-off

An employer is ordinarily entitled to set-off against a contractor's claim for payment his own claim for defective work.

There was a line of cases, commencing with *Dawnays v FG Minter and Trollope and Colls* [1971] 1 WLR 1205 that held that this set-off did not exist where the contractor sought certified sums. The certificate was said to be like a cheque, such that set-off was not available against it. *Dawnays v Minter* was overruled by the House of Lords in *Gilbert-Ash (Northern) Ltd v Modern Engineering (Bristol) Ltd* [1974] AC 689. Some care is needed, however, when looking at the *Gilbert-Ash* case, since it concerns the construction of a particular set-off clause in the standard sub-contract form of the Bovis group of companies; Lords Reid and Morris of Borth-y-Gest each thought that *Dawnays v Minter* was correct upon its particular facts. The principle that emerges, however, is that there is no rule of law that certificates are to be treated like cheques, without any right of set-off.

In ordinary cases, where there is no certification, the same principle applies. The contractor must give credit for the cost of remedying defects but may recover the balance either at trial or under Ord 14.

In practice it is frequently desirable for a contractor to offer to remedy any defects that he accepts as his responsibility; the cost to the contractor of doing so is almost certainly going to be less than the price of another contractor. If the employer does not take up such offer, he may have failed to mitigate his loss. In appropriate circumstances the contractor may consider a without prejudice funding agreement; see p 162.

(e) Limitation

As in the case of an employer's claim for defects, contractor's claims for payment usually erode gradually rather than suddenly become statute barred. Contractors' rights to payment generally start eroding about six years after the date of commencement of work.

Where there is a limitation danger concerning a contract with an arbitration clause, the contractor should protect his position by issuing a writ *and* serving an arbitration notice. Where the architect issues an unsatisfactory final certificate, the contractor should issue a writ and/or serve an arbitration notice immediately.

(f) Claim documents

Contractors sometimes spend much time and/or money in the preparation of claim documents that are frequently lengthy claims for extensions of time and payment by way of loss and expense. These claims often have the relevant documents appended to them. In many cases, such documents are prepared, presented and rejected before the prospect of litigation emerges. Sometimes the lawyers are consulted before any claim document is prepared. In long and complicated cases, the claim documents can be of great use, not only to provide the architect and quantity surveyor with the information they need to perform their functions but also to append to the pleadings.

Claim documents are almost invariably prepared by persons qualified or experienced as quantity surveyors. It is usually not possible or practicable for the lawyers to write or extensively re-write such claims but it is often useful for the lawyers to go through the claim documents and make suggestions before they are presented or incorporated into pleadings.

3 Claims by sub-contractors for payment

From a sub-contractor's point of view the main contractor stands in the position of employer and the same considerations as set out above apply. Additionally, there are two circumstances where a sub-contractor may be entitled to look to the employer for payment directly where the JCT contract is used.

First, there is a procedure under Clause 35.13 of the main contract whereby the main contractor is obliged to provide the architect with reasonable proof that he has paid every nominated sub-contractor the amount he is directed so to do. If the contractor is unable to provide such proof, the nominated sub-contractor may be entitled to direct payment under Clause 35.13.5.

Secondly, where the main contract is determined by the employer under Clause 27 then the employer *may* pay any supplier or sub-contractor, whether nominated or not, for any materials or goods delivered for works executed for the purposes of the contract insofar as the price thereof has not already been paid by the contractor (Clause 27.4.2.2). This position does not apply where the determination occurs by reason of the bankruptcy of the contractor or of a winding up order being made (Clause 27.4.2.1).

4 Papers

Building contract litigation frequently involves paper-work on a huge scale. Even comparatively small contracts—in the region of say £50,000—can produce enough paper-work to fill several lever-arch files; in larger cases the paper-work can run into many dozen such files.

At what stage in litigation should the parties and their advisers read the documentation? It is often a counsel of perfection to read all the papers before taking any steps in contemplation of litigation. That is frequently impractical and in large cases it may be impractical for any one person ever to read all of the papers; but it is essential to separate the important items.

Where the dispute concerns defects, it is likely to be important to read the following documents:

 (i) the documents that set out the basic contractual obligation;
 (ii) the specification, drawings and/or bills of quantities which set out and describe the work which the contractor was obliged to do;
 (iii) correspondence between the parties or their agents with regard to the defects;
 (iv) any reports upon the defects; and
 (v) the Building Regulations or any other requirements (which may or may not be included in the contract papers) as to the standard of the works. (It is often extremely relevant whether the defects alleged satisfy such statutory requirements, and it may well be worthwhile obtaining and reading the relevant parts of these documents.)

Where the claim is a claim for payment upon a certificate made under a building contract, it is usually sufficient merely to look at the contract documentation and the certificates themselves in the first instance. The form of pleading in such a case is simple, and there is frequently little point in wasting time considering the matters that the architect and/or surveyor would have considered before making their certificate.

The case of a claim by a builder for sums due under a contract where there is no certificate upon which he relies can pose much more difficult problems. The claim frequently contains elements relating to extra work, delay, loss of profit, liability to sub-contractors and so on. The documents that are likely to be material to the claim are often very substantial, and would include:

  (i) the contract documentation;
 (ii) the specification, drawings and/or bills of quantities which set out the original contract work;
(iii) architect's instructions and confirmations of verbal instructions;
 (iv) day work sheets;
  (v) the site diary;
 (vi) the correspondence;
(vii) interim applications, interim certifications and payments;
(viii) prime cost records;
 (ix) materials invoices;
  (x) sub-contractor claims;
 (xi) profit and loss accounts; and
(xii) site meeting minutes.

The list goes on. It is often impractical to read all of these documents before proceeding to make a claim and to embark upon litigation or arbitration. It is frequently necessary to make an assessment of the position and then hope that the assessment will in due course be supported if necessary by the paper-work. How much can reasonably be taken on trust has much to do with the legal expertise of the person making the assessments but it is often well worthwhile making sample excursions into the above sources of paper-work in order to form a view as to the support that it would give at trial. This is often unnecessary before issuing the writ where some form of claim document has already been prepared; it may well be wiser to get proceedings in motion as soon as possible; but there are three dangers arising out of not reading the papers in such a case:

  (1) It is almost impossible to make reliable practical decisions as to the interlocutory steps to be pursued without having read the material papers. Most cases have strengths and weaknesses and the ability of a party to play upon its strong points and distract attention from its weak points is paramount.

  (2) There is a limit to which a party can rely safely upon its right to amend. Where there is an Ord 14 claim, the pleadings ought to be in reasonable order from the outset. Where a case is going to trial, a party will suffer real prejudice if it has not got its pleadings reasonably in order, say, a month before trial when it delivers its papers to counsel to advise upon evidence.

  (3) The vast majority of building contract cases are settled. It is extremely difficult to settle a case effectively without know-

ing the likely result at trial with some degree of certainty, and this almost always involves reading a substantial part of the material paper-work.

Claims by contractors for an extension of time follow much the same pattern as claims by contractors for sums due other than pursuant to a certificate; but in addition, if there is a contract programme (which would usually be set out as a bar chart), this is essential reading. There are innumerable systems of diagrammatically representing delay and reconciling programmed operations with actual progress. It is extremely important to consider and understand these documents; they are practically the only way of separating the relevant events from the irrelevant events.

5 Bar charts

A bar chart is a diagrammatic illustration showing the order and duration of different operations with a project. Where a bar chart shows the *intended* sequence of operations it is usually known as a programme. Where it shows the *actual* sequence it is usually known as a progress chart. Where it contains an analysis of which delays have caused an overall delay it is usually known as a critical path analysis.

Figure 1 shows a programme for an hypothetical project to be completed within twelve weeks. It has the following hypothetical features:

Operation 1: *Foundations.* The foundations require to be completed before the rest of the work can proceed.

Operation 2: *Car park.* The car park may be constructed at any time independently of the rest of the building works. Because the construction of the car park requires the use of some of the same plant as the foundations it follows on immediately after the foundations work.

Operation 3: *Framework.* The frame of the building cannot be commenced until the foundations are complete, and itself needs to be completed before either the roofing or the brickwork and blockwork can be commenced.

Operation 4: *Roofing.* The roofing cannot be commenced until the framework is complete, but may be carried out at the same time as the brickwork and blockwork. The roofing must be completed before the painting work can commence.

Operation 5: *Brickwork and blockwork.* The brickwork and blockwork cannot be commenced until the framework is complete, and must itself be complete before the painting can start.

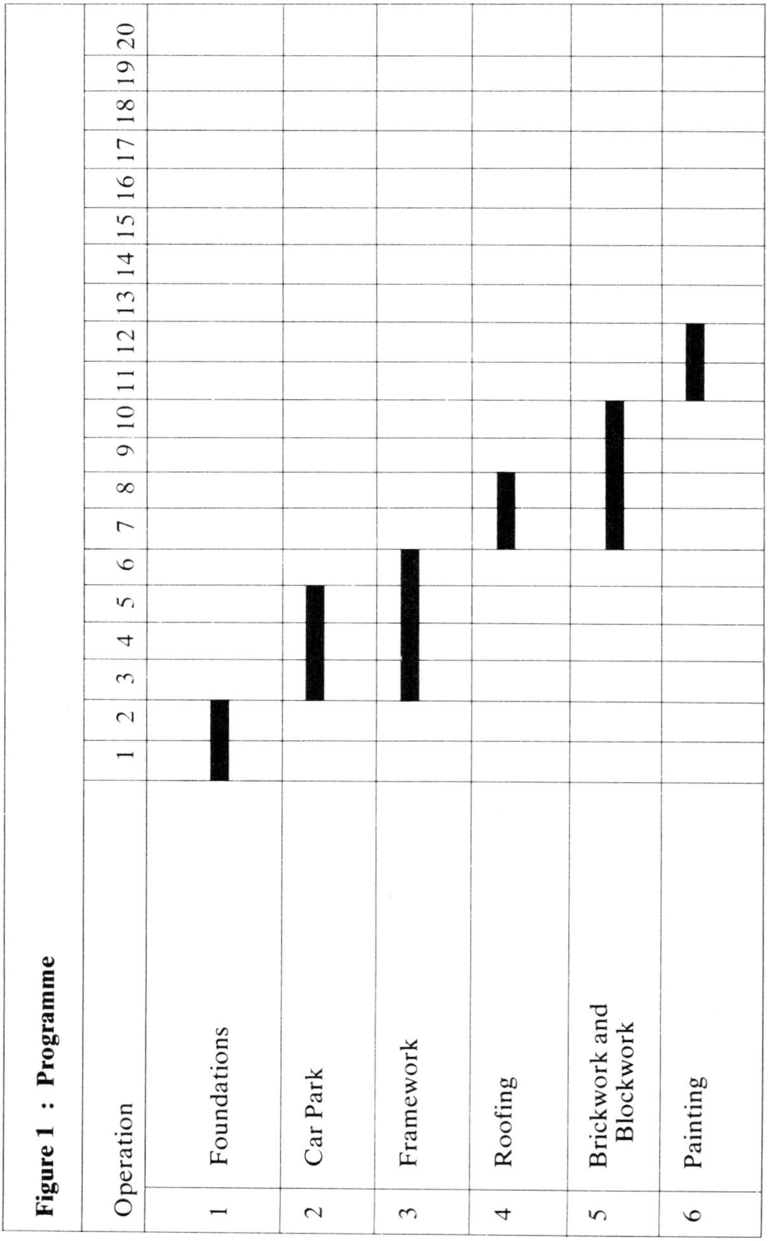

Figure 1 : Programme

Operation		1	2	3	4	5	6	7	8	9	10	11	12	13	14	15	16	17	18	19	20
1	Foundations	■																			
2	Car Park			■																	
3	Framework			■			■														
4	Roofing								■												
5	Brickwork and Blockwork										■										
6	Painting												■								

Figure 2 : Progress Chart

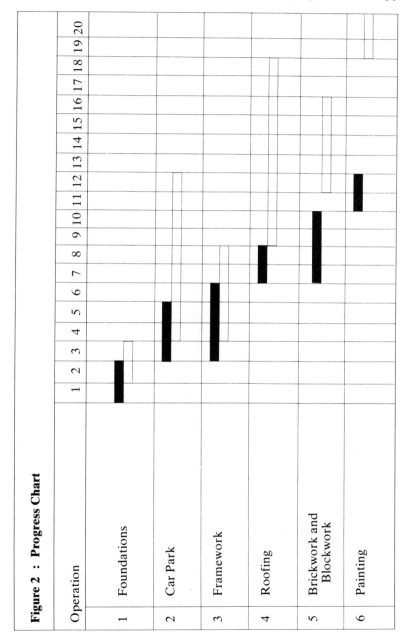

Operation		1	2	3	4	5	6	7	8	9	10	11	12	13	14	15	16	17	18	19	20
1	Foundations																				
2	Car Park																				
3	Framework																				
4	Roofing																				
5	Brickwork and Blockwork																				
6	Painting																				

Figure 3 : Critical Path Analysis

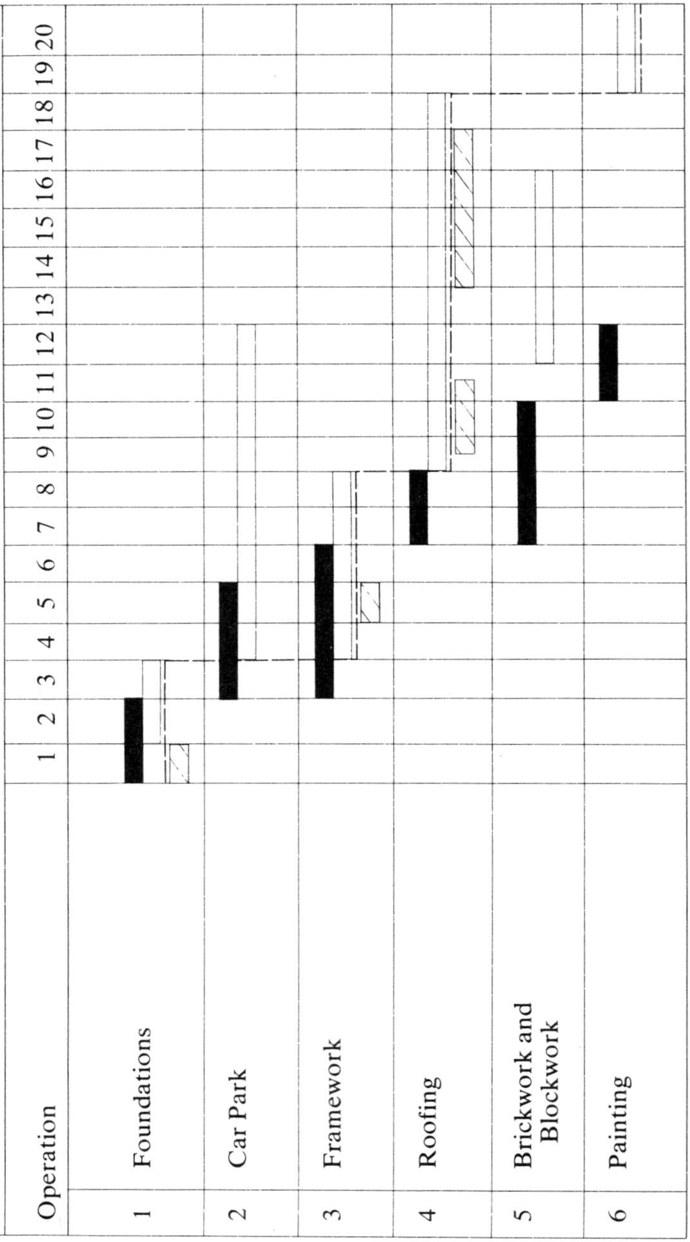

Operation		1	2	3	4	5	6	7	8	9	10	11	12	13	14	15	16	17	18	19	20
1	Foundations																				
2	Car Park																				
3	Framework																				
4	Roofing																				
5	Brickwork and Blockwork																				
6	Painting																				

Operation 6: *Painting.* Because of its nature, the painting work cannot be started until all the other work within the building is complete.

It can be seen that the programme represents a plan for the execution of the work as quickly as possible. There are some operations which are envisaged as being on the critical path, that is to say that any delay in those operations will, prima facie, lead to a delay in the completion of the project as a whole. In this case, the critical operations are foundations, framework, brickwork and blockwork and painting. The car park is an example of an operation that is not critical; it would not delay completion if it were delayed (for example) from weeks 3 to 5 inclusive to weeks 9 to 11 inclusive.

Figure 2 is a hypothetical progress chart. The black bars show the programmed sequence and the white bars show the actual time of the carrying out of the operation. The explanation for the delays is as follows:

Operation 1: *Foundations.* The plant which the contractor required to execute the foundation was late in arriving on site and a week was wasted as a result. Once the foundations were started they took two weeks as envisaged.

Operation 2: *Car Park.* The car park took nine weeks instead of the three weeks envisaged. The reason for this was partly exceptionally heavy rainfall in weeks 9, 10 and 11, and partly because the contractor did not have enough workmen on that operation.

Operation 3: *Framework.* This operation took five weeks instead of four weeks, because in week 5 the architect issued a variation requiring certain changes in the details of the framework.

Operation 4: *Roofing.* This operation took ten weeks instead of the two weeks envisaged. Of the additional eight weeks, six weeks were attributable to the contractor not having enough men on the operation, and two weeks were attributable to the exceptionally heavy rain in weeks 9 to 11.

Operation 5: *Brickwork and blockwork.* This operation took five weeks instead of the four weeks envisaged. The reason for this was the delay by the architect in giving the necessary instructions as to detailing.

Operation 6: *Painting.* The painting work took two weeks as envisaged.

It can readily be seen that without the aid of a bar chart, it would be extremely difficult to show which of these delays had contributed and to what extent to the overall delay of eight weeks. In a complex case, where there may be fifty separate operations bearing relationships to each other, the problem of working without a bar chart would be greatly amplified.

Figure 3 shows a typical critical path analysis. The dotted line traces the critical path from commencement to completion. It shows that the delay in the construction of the car park was irrelevant to the time of completion, and it also shows that roofing has taken the place of brickwork and blockwork as the critical operation between the completion of the framework and the commencement of painting.

Critical path analyses are sometimes adorned with glorious polychromatic representations of such concepts as critical delay, non-critical delay, delay carried forward, float periods, and so on. The important representation is the apportionment of the total delay between various quarters. In figure 3 the hatched bar makes such an apportionment as follows:

Operation 1: Foundations — Delay in arrival of plant		1 week
Operation 3: Framework — Architect's instruction		1 week
Operation 4: Roofing — Bad weather		2 weeks
Contractor's delay		4 weeks
		8 weeks

It is often remarkably difficult in critical path analyses to make the individually analysed delays add up to the total delays. This difficulty often arises out of 'float periods', an example of which occurs in this example in the roofing operation. It can be seen from Figure 1 that the roofing operation had a float period of two weeks, that is to say that the roofing operation could be delayed by two weeks before it would delay the commencement of painting and thereby delay completion as a whole. Accordingly, two weeks out of the total delay of eight weeks in Operation 4 was not critical. In the analysis at Figure 3, this two weeks has been deducted from the contractor's delay of six weeks, but arguably it could in whole or in part be deducted from the delay caused by bad weather in that operation.

If the contract were in the standard JCT form, the result of the analysis would be as follows:

Extension of time — The contractor is entitled to an extension of time of one week for the architect's instruction with regard to the framework and a further extension of two weeks having regard to the exceptionally adverse weather conditions affecting the roofing work. The contractor is accordingly entitled to a total extension of time of three weeks but must pay liquidated damages upon the balance of delay of five weeks.

Loss and Expense—The contractor has a prolongation claim for the one week delay incurred by reason of the architect's instruction as to framework. Although it did not delay completion, the contractor may also have a disruption claim resulting from the delay by the architect in giving instructions with regard to brickwork and blockworks. The contractor is not entitled to any loss and expense caused as a result of bad weather.

Chapter 6

Who to Sue

The list of dramatis personae in building contract litigation can be lengthy. Apart from the employer and the contractor, there is often an architect and/or surveyor and a number of sub-contractors. Sometimes there are specialist designers, receivers, bondsmen and insurers. The local authority is charged with enforcing the building regulations. There may be suppliers whose products are at fault.

All these are capable of attracting liability, and a plaintiff is sometimes faced with a wide choice of targets. The following analysis is not intended to provide a code for making such a choice, nor is it intended to be exhaustive. It is, however, intended to assist in an orderly review of some of the more common causes of action.

1 Claims by contractors for payment

(a) Against the employer

Most commonly, of course, the contractor's claim for payment will be against the employer with whom he has entered into his contract. The claim may be for payment under the contract, in quasi-contract, or for breach of the contract by the employer.

Ordinarily, there is no difficulty in identifying the employer, whether the employer be an individual, a company or a partnership. The ordinary rules of contract law apply. It sometimes happens, however, that the contractor's claim is in quasi-contract where, for example, the terms of the proposed contract are never settled with sufficient certainty as to create a binding contract. In these circumstances, the contractor's claim in quasi-contract may be against a different person from the person who proposed to enter into the contract. The person who is liable upon a claim in quasi-contract is the person for whom and at whose request the works are carried out.

(b) Against the architect

It frequently happens that the negotiations for building works are carried out by either an architect, a surveyor, an estate agent, or by some other professional person. In such circumstances it sometimes happens, more usually by accident than by design, that such a

64

person himself incurs a contractual liability. Such a liability can arise where the architect or other professional person personally enters into the contract without disclosing the existence of a principal or expressly excluding his liability (*Beigtheil & Young* v *Stewart*(1900) 16 TLR 177). An architect may further be liable for breach of warranty of authority on the basis that one who expressly or impliedly warrants that he has the authority of another is liable for breach of warranty of authority to any person to whom the warranty is made and who suffers damage by acting on the faith thereof, if in fact he had no such authority (*Collen* v *Wright*(1857) 8 E & B 647). It is not necessary for a contractor to show fraud or negligence to found such a claim; in *Collen* v *Wright* it was said:

> 'The fact that the professed agent honestly thinks that he has authority affects the moral character of his act; but his moral innocence, so far as the person whom he has induced to contract is concerned, in no way aids such person or alleviates the inconvenience and damage which he sustains. The obligation arising in such a case is well expressed by saying that a person, professing to contract as agent for another, impliedly if not expressly, undertakes to or promises the person who enters into the contract upon the faith of the professed agent being duly authorised, that the authority which he professes to have does in point of fact exist.'

In practice it is often difficult for a contractor to know what measure of damage flows from a breach of warranty of authority by an architect, especially where the lack of authority represents a part only of the contractor's claim for payment. Where there is doubt as to whether and to what extent an employer will seek to defend himself by pointing to lack of authority in the architect, the contractor's prudent course is to join both the employer and the architect as joint defendants.

In a formal building contract, where the architect is appointed as a certifier, the architect has a duty both to the employer and to the contractor to act fairly, and it appears that the architect may be liable to the contractor in damages if he fails to do so (see *Sutcliffe* v *Thackrah* [1974] AC 727 HL and *Arenson* v *Casson Beckman Rutley & Co* [1977] AC 405 HL).

(c) Against a liquidator

Where an employer is a limited company and is the subject of a winding-up order or the appointment of a provisional liquidator, no action can be proceeded with or commenced against the company except by leave of the court (Companies Act 1948, s 231). Where the contractor has a claim for payment against the company, it should prove in the winding up for such claim.

Where, notwithstanding s 231, an employer company in liquidation brings an action against a contractor, the contractor may, without the leave of the court, set up a cross demand for liquidated or unliquidated damages as a set-off to reduce or extinguish the company's claim (*Langley Constructions (Brixham) Ltd* v *Wells* [1969] 1 WLR 503).

(d) Against a receiver

Where a receiver is appointed of an employer company, there is no prohibition on a contractor bringing a claim against the company for a pre-existing debt, although the contractor may wish to consider carefully whether the cost of instituting or continuing proceedings is worthwhile.

Contracts made by a company and current at the date of the appointment of the receiver are not binding on the receiver personally unless they become binding by a novation (*Moss Steamship Co* v *Whinney* [1912] AC 254).

(e) Against sub-contractors and suppliers

Where part of the contractor's cost of carrying out building works results from the faults of his sub-contractors or suppliers, the terms of the contract usually prevent the contractor from recovering such part of the cost from the employer. He must look to the sub-contractor or supplier in default.

2 Claims by employers for defects

Sometimes an employer's claim in respect of building defects is entirely straightforward and there is no doubt as to the liability of the contractor and the contractor's ability to meet that liability. In many other cases, however, the contractor may be able to raise some form of defence or there may be doubts as to his solvency. In these circumstances the employer should consider whether to make a claim against some other party either alone, or as a co-defendant.

In addition to a claim for breach of contract against the contractor, an employer may also be able to bring claims in negligence, breach of statutory duty, or under the Defective Premises Act 1972. These other avenues are available not only to the original employer under the building contract but also to a subsequent owner of the building. The comments that follow are also of relevance with regard to the position of a subsequent owner.

(a) Against landlords and tenants

The employer is sometimes in the position of landlord and/or tenant of the site. If there is a lease involved, it is worthwhile considering the terms of the lease to see who is responsible for the physical state of the building. This consideration not only affects the issue of whether an employer should take it upon himself to enforce any rights against any party but also the question of in whose name the proceedings should be brought.

(b) Against the contractor

The liability of a contractor under a contract is usually absolute, and if so there is no need for the employer to show negligence on the part of the contractor. For this reason, the employer's strongest claim against the contractor is usually for breach of the building contract. There are, however, certain circumstances where the employer can and should avail himself of other courses of action against the contractor.

It may be that the employer for some particular circumstances such as limitation is unable to pursue the contractor in contract. The employer may have sold on to a subsequent owner such that the subsequent owner has no contractual nexus with the contractor. In these circumstances the employer or subsequent owner may be able to sue in negligence or for breach of statutory duty with regard to building regulations (*Anns* v *Merton* BC (1977) 5 BLR 1).

Employers and subsequent owners may also have a claim against the contractor under the Defective Premises Act 1972.

(c) Against sub-contractors and suppliers

The basic rule is that an employer has no direct contractual nexus with a sub-contractor, and the chain of liability flows 'down the line'. There are, however, various inroads into this general rule.

Firstly, the principles enunciated in the recent cases on negligence in building matters, and in particular *Anns* v *Merton* [1978] AC 728, *Batty* v *Metropolitan Property Realisation* [1978] QB 554, *Independent Broadcasting Authority* v *EMI* (1981) 14 BLR 1, appear to open the way for an employer to sue a sub-contractor or a supplier in negligence, at any rate where a health or safety factor is present. That area of the law seems to be still in a state of flux, and it will remain to be seen over the coming years whether and in what circumstances an employer can obtain a remedy against a sub-contractor directly in negligence. As it stands, the claim is frequently made, and is usually taken seriously, especially in the light of the *IBA* case.

In the cases where is applies, the Defective Premises Act 1972 is capable of providing an employer with a direct course of action against a sub-contractor.

Where there are negotiations between a sub-contractor or supplier and the building owner or his architect, there may upon the facts arise a collateral warranty on the part of the sub-contractor or supplier as to his ability to perform. The consideration in such a case is usually the employer causing the nomination of that sub-contractor or supplier as in *Shanklin Pier Co Ltd* v *Detel Products* [1951] 2 KB 854. The continuing importance of the collateral warranty was vividly illustrated by the Court of Appeal in *Esso* v *Mardon* [1976] QB 801.

Under the JCT system, that collateral warranty is reduced into a formal agreement between the employer and the nominated sub-contractor in the standard form of agreement NSC/2. That warranty relates to design matters, the selection of materials and goods and the satisfaction of any performance specification or requirement; the warranty does not extend to workmanship in the ordinary sense of the word.

(d) Against the architect

Where a building owner employs an architect, the architect usually has obligations that include, inter alia, the design of the works and the supervision of the work carried out by the builder. Very often, the architect stipulates that the conditions of his emp-loyment should be RIBA Conditions of Engagement, but these conditions do not throw any great light upon the nature of these duties. In ordinary cases, the duties of design and supervision are not absolute, but are merely duties to exercise a reasonable degree of professional care and skill.

In practical terms, it is often very difficult for a building owner to know whether a building defect arises out of a failure of the architect to make a proper design or out of the failure of the contractor properly to execute the design. Likewise, it is often difficult to know whether a workmanship failure by the contractor could have been prevented by proper supervision by the architect. This difficulty can have especial importance in that a building owner often needs to know whether to regard the architect as friend or foe in litigation against the contractor. A course that building owners sometimes take in these circumstances is to obtain the agreement of the architect not to plead limitation and to make plain to the architect that, if litigation against the contractor proves unsuccess-ful by reason of the contractor showing the default to be that of the architect, the building owner reserves his right to pursue a claim against the architect. Usually, the architect will be insured through a professional indemnity policy, and such arrangements require the consent of the architect's insurer if the policy is not to be avoided.

The above remarks also apply to the position of engineers and quantity surveyors who undertake the same functions as architects.

(e) Against the local authority

Local authorities have a statutory function of enforcing by-laws that relate to building, and while it is not the local authorities' obligation to inspect at every stage it is their duty to give proper consideration to the question of whether they should inspect or not. The local authority can be liable in tort where it fails to give proper consideration to that question or, having assumed the duty of actually inspecting the building, it fails to exercise reasonable care to ensure that the applicable by-laws are complied with (*Anns* v *Merton* [1978] AC 728).

Liability may attach to the local authority notwithstanding that the architect may be primarily liable (*Acrecrest* v *Hattrell* (1979) 252 EG 1107); but the liability is not an absolute one and the building inspector is not expected to exercise the skill of a professionally qualified expert (*Stewart* v *East Cambridgeshire District Council* (1979) 252 EG 1105).

(f) Against the vendor or developer

Where a person has acquired his property from a vendor, especially if that vendor is a developer, a liability may attach to the vendor on account of the particular circumstances (*Batty* v *Metropolitan Property Realisations* [1978] QB 554).

(g) Against a bondsman

Employers sometimes require that the contractor procure the issue of a performance bond or other guarantee from an insurance company or other financial institution. Such bonds are frequently required in the case of engineering contracts in the ICE form.

These bonds or guarantees are frequently limited in amount, often to ten per cent of the contract price, and they are in the nature of a guarantee on the part of the bondsman that the contractor will perform his contractual obligations.

(h) Against the contractor's architect

In the case of a design and build contract, where the employer does not employ his own professional men to design the work, the contractor is responsible for the design of the work as well as the execution of that design. Frequently, the main contractor sub-contracts a part of the design work, sometimes together with a part of the construction work, to his own professional agent or specialist sub-contractor. In such a case, the designer is under an obligation in contract to the main contractor. In some circumstances this obligation may be an absolute obligation for fitness of purpose independently of whether or not the designer is negligent (*Greaves* v *Baynham Meikle* [1975] 1 WLR 1095). In addition to this contractual liability may also have a liability in negligence to the employer (*ITA* v *EMI & BIC Ltd* (1981) 14 BLR 1).

Chapter 7

To Arbitrate or to Litigate?

Contrary to popular belief in the construction industry, arbitration in building contract matters is generally slower, more expensive and less certain than High Court litigation. Many people in the industry take the view that it is essential to have their dispute heard by someone with a working knowledge of building contracts and the practices that are prevalent in the industry. They often lean towards arbitration as a means of achieving that end. They frequently fail to take account of the Official Referees Court, which is almost invariably the court within the High Court that takes building contract matters, at any rate in London. The Official Referees are appointed from leading counsel and spend a great deal of their time hearing disputes about building contracts. They have therefore come to acquire a detailed working knowledge of the construction industry in much the same way as the professional arbitrators, who are almost always qualified architects.

There is another common view in the industry that arbitrators are able to bring to bear more common sense than High Court judges and are able to 'cut through the red tape'. This is also largely fallacious. Where an arbitrator takes it into his head to 'cut through the red tape' his decision will very frequently be appealable in the courts. Sometimes it will go further. For example, in the recent case of *Modern Engineering (Bristol) Limited* v *C Miskin & Son Limited* [1981] 2 Lloyd's Rep 135 the arbitrator was faced with a point of law as to whether an architect's certificate could be reviewed. The arbitrator evidently thought that he knew the answer to that point, and he made an interim formal award without listening to full legal argument. That attempt to shortcut the proceedings backfired. The arbitrator was removed for misconduct under the Arbitration Act 1950, s 21(1), and his award was set aside under s 23(2).

Notwithstanding these matters, many building contracts contain an arbitration agreement, whereby the parties pre-agree to refer any disputes that may arise to arbitration.

It is a great mistake for a claimant to assume that because the contract contains an arbitration clause he is necessarily bound to pursue his claim in arbitration rather than in the courts. Likewise, a defendant to High Court proceedings should consider whether to attempt to have the High Court proceedings stayed under the Arbitration Act 1950, s 4, so that the matter may proceed in arbitration. Similarly, a respondent who is served with an arbitration notice ought to consider whether he would be better off if the matter were dealt with in the courts.

This chapter then will provide guidance both for the pursuer and the pursued. In High Court litigation the parties are known as plaintiff and defendant; in arbitration proceedings the parties are known as claimant and respondent. In this chapter the terminology is used interchangeably according to the context.

Before examining the detailed considerations that are likely to influence the choice between arbitration and litigation there are three points of major importance relating to: limitation, Order 14 and taking a step in the action. Failure to have regard to these points may seriously prejudice a party's position.

(i) *Limitation:* If a plaintiff has reason to believe that the limitation period may expire before the determination of the dispute, then he must remember that for limitation purposes in arbitrations the test is whether the arbitration is commenced before the expiration of the limitation period, be it six years of twelve years. For these purposes, the arbitration commences when one party serves on the other a notice requiring him to appoint or agree to the appointment of an arbitrator or (where the arbitration agreement names or designates the arbitrator) requiring him to submit the dispute to the persons so named or designated (Limitation Act 1980, s 34). Accordingly, for protective purposes it is necessary not only to issue a writ but also to commence arbitration proceedings by the service of a formal arbitration notice (which can be so worded as to make it clear that it is merely protective and without prejudice to a contention that the dispute ought to be dealt with in the court, see p 148). If the plaintiff merely issues a writ without serving an arbitration notice then there is a danger that the defendant may successfully take out a summons staying the court proceedings under the Arbitration Act 1950, s 4. By that time, an arbitration notice may already be out of time. Likewise, if a claimant merely pursues the arbitration without issuing a writ, then he may subsequently find that, for all sorts of reasons, he is later compelled to proceed in the court and it may be too late for him to issue a writ.

(ii) *Order 14:* The second central point to bear in mind is that litigation and arbitration are not mutually exclusive. If a part of the claim is within the scope of Ord 14, then it is open for the claimant to first sue and recover under Ord 14 the indisputable part of the claim, and to pursue the balance in arbitration (see p 113).

(iii) *Taking a step in the proceedings:* A party who is served with an arbitration notice usually has some time in hand if he wants the proceedings heard in the court. The arbitration does not commence (except for limitation purposes) until an arbitrator is appointed, and (unless both parties agree upon a mutually acceptable arbitrator) it usually takes some time for the claimant to procure that appointment. Arbitrators rarely accept any appointment until their identity is known to both parties. On the other hand, a defendant to High Court proceedings must move swiftly if he wishes to have the action stayed for arbitration. He must issue his summons under the Arbitration Act 1950 s 4, before delivering any pleadings or taking any other steps in the proceedings. Even a time summons can be fatal. Such a defendant must, therefore, decide very rapidly whether he wishes to issue a section 4 summons, and if he does he should not delay. A further discussion of the Arbitration Act 1950, s 4, and what constitutes a step in the proceedings appears at p 108.

It is beyond the scope of this book to consider in detail the wording of the arbitration clauses in current use. Suffice it to say that arbitration clauses of the type in *Scott* v *Avery* (1856) 5 HLC 811 are rare in building contracts (ie it is rare to see a provision in a building contract arbitration clause that the making of an award by an arbitrator shall be a condition precedent to the right to bring an action in the courts). It is also worth noting that the usual arbitration clauses are widely drawn, and in particular the JCT arbitration clause (which appears at Article 5 of the 1980 Edition) is likely to cover almost any dispute between the parties to a building contract that relates to the works.

1 Agreements relating to existing disputes

In building contract matters, arbitrations arise in one of two ways. Usually they arise out of a pre-agreement between the parties to refer to arbitration any disputes that may arise out of their dealings. Arbitration clauses containing such pre-agreement appear (usually at the end) in practically every standard form of building contract and very frequently appear at the end of builders' standard terms and conditions. Very frequently, the parties to the contract will not even notice the existence of the arbitration clause. If they do, and if it is then their desire for any dispute to be promptly resolved by arbitration proceedings, there is still no guarantee that that desire will subsist once a dispute has become apparent. More likely, the respondent would prefer to put off the dispute for as long as possible. Arbitrations are particularly suitable for respondents who wish to avoid the resolution of a dispute.

Alternatively, contracting parties who encounter a bona fide dispute during the course of their dealings may agree to refer that dispute to arbitration. Usually in such cases neither party is seeking to evade its liabilities. The parties simply disagree as to some matter and wish their disagreement to be resolved as quickly as possible by an independent person so that they can resume their business. The contract may yet be in progress and the parties may not wish to sour their working relationship by court proceedings.

Such latter agreements are generally likely to involve different principles from the principles involved in pre-agreements to arbitrate. Agreements to arbitrate existing disputes are frequently accompanied by further agreement as to the choice of arbitrator, the time by which the arbitrator will be asked to make his award, and so on. If there is a genuinely reciprocal desire to resolve the dispute, the arbitration is likely to be efficient and successful as a forum. Many of the factors referred to in this chapter do not apply but there are some particular dangers that a party in dispute should be warned against. In particular:

(i) Parties in dispute should be warned against selecting an inexperienced arbitrator. It is frequently thought by non-lawyers that the main requirement of an arbitrator is knowledge of the subject matter of the dispute. In fact, it requires experience of arbitrations to act effectively as an arbitrator and except in the very simplest of cases it is a dangerous practice to appoint as arbitrator a person who does not have adequate experience as such.

(ii) There is a difference between experts and arbitrators, and clients may require advice as to which is preferable.

(iii) If the dispute relates only to the construction of a document (and the standard contracts are full of scope for such dispute) remember that that dispute can be resolved pursuant to the issue of a construction summons in the High Court. The parties may not wish to involve the court at all, but it may be that they are simply unaware that it is possible to have a High Court judge construe a document without all the palaver of pleadings and discovery.

2 Costs

Some people fondly imagine that arbitrations are free of the enormous legal costs that court actions involve. This is not true. It is almost certain that each side in a building contract arbitration of any substance will require legal representation in exactly the same way as if the matter were proceeding in the courts. Furthermore, the arbitrator almost always has the power to order payment of the costs in the same way as if the matter were proceeding in the High

Court (Arbitration Act 1950, s 18(1)) and the arbitrator must exercise that power in accordance with judicial principles (*Donald Campbell & Co* v *Pollack* [1927] AC 732 HL).

On the whole (and there is no hard and fast rule) the costs of an arbitration tend to be higher than the costs of a similar High Court action. There are two main reasons for this.

First, the costs of the arbitration itself (as opposed to the costs of the parties) are likely to be greater. At the time of writing the fee on the issue of a writ for an unliquidated claim or a liquidated claim in excess of £2,000 is £40. A further fee of £20 is payable on transfer to the Official Referee's Court or setting down for trial. No other fees are payable by the parties in respect of the time spent by the judge, the use of the court office, the use of the court room or the tape recording of proceedings by the mechanical recording department. In the case of arbitration proceedings, however, the parties must pay the arbitrator for his time spent on the arbitration (the current rate for a senior experienced arbitrator is about £50 per hour), must pay the hire charge for an arbitration room (which is likely to be at least £60 per day or part of a day), and may feel it necessary for a record of the proceedings to be kept by mechanical tape recording or by shorthand writers. These expenses (or a proportion of them) are frequently payable even if they are not used because of a last minute settlement.

Secondly, arbitrators generally do not exercise the same control over arbitrations, either at interlocutory stages or at trial, that the High Court exercises in litigation. This is partly because of a wariness, understandable in a non-lawyer, and partly because they do not enjoy the same inherent jurisdiction as does the High Court. This means (*a*) that arbitration proceedings are frequently more protracted, which plainly involves greater cost for the parties, and (*b*) the more complex procedure of applying to the court in relation to an arbitration can involve additional expense.

3 Speed

There are a variety of factors that affect whether arbitration is likely to be quicker or slower than litigation in the courts.

There are some arbitrators who are particularly conscious of the need to resolve disputes speedily, especially in cases where the parties remain actively in contract and need their disputes resolved rapidly in order to proceed with their dealings. In those cases, arbitration can be substantially quicker. Likewise, where the only substantial point in issue is a short technical point, then again arbitration can frequently be substantially quicker than High Court litigation.

In cases where the parties are no longer actively in a contractual relationship with each other, as for example where there is a long list of alleged defects, or a complex loss and expense or damages claim, then litigation is generally more rapid than arbitration. Experienced arbitrators frequently have diaries booked many months in advance, and where a lengthy trial of weeks rather than days is required then the trial date which they will give is frequently more distant than would be the case in the Official Referees Court.

Where it is in the interests of one party to procrastinate, that party will have a greater opportunity for procrastination in arbitration than in the High Court. The procedure for enforcing orders as to discovery and as to pleadings is more cumbersome in arbitration and takes correspondingly longer.

4 Third parties

It is a feature of arbitrations that they result from an agreement between two parties to submit differences inter se to an arbitrator. That arbitrator does not have the same jurisdiction as would the High Court over any other party.

Multi-party litigation is particularly common in building contract disputes. Where an employer alleges delay as against a main contractor, the main contractor will very frequently want to pass on the whole or part of the delay claim to one or more of his sub-contractors. Likewise, where an employer alleges that a main contractor's work is defective, the main contractor may well claim that the error originated from the architect, the structural engineer, or from one of his sub-contractors. Some part of the blame can frequently be passed on to the local authority if it negligently failed in its exercise of its duty to inspect the works (*Acrecrest* v *Hattrell* (1979) 252 EG 1107) where a contractor claims entitlement or further entitlement to be paid from the employer, it may be because of an existing or anticipated claim by a sub-contractor. It is not unknown for the number of parties in substantial High Court building contract litigation to pass comfortably into double figures.

There are many advantages of joining all the relevant parties into the same action, as is only possible in the courts. It avoids duplication of cost, it reduces the possibility of different findings upon the same subject matter, and it reduces the risk of a party being called upon to meet a substantial claim before he is able to recover in respect of the same subject matter.

Arbitration agreements sometimes contain complex machinery designed to go some way to overcoming this defect in the arbitration process. Article 5.4 of the JCT contract contains such a provision.

The terms of such a provision should be carefully considered in appropriate circumstances.

5 Limitation

It is possible for an action to be statute-barred for the purpose of court proceedings but not for the purpose of arbitration, or vice versa. For High Court proceedings the test is whether the plaintiff has issued his writ within the limitation period. For the purposes of an arbitration, however, the test is whether or not the claimant has, within the limitation period, served on the respondent a notice requiring him to appoint or agree to the appointment of an arbitrator or (where the arbitration agreement names or designates the arbitrator) requiring him to submit the dispute to the persons so named or designated (Limitation Act 1980, s 34).

The limitation consideration when choosing between litigation and arbitration is often very complex. Limitation in building contract matters is almost always an imprecise science (see p 158) and frequently the effect of limitation is to erode a party's case in stages rather at one fell swoop. Furthermore, a plaintiff who has issued proceedings within the limitation period but continues to litigate after that time is in a vulnerable position in at least two respects:

  (i) it is very common for building contract matters to be inadequately pleaded in the first case; to amend pleadings after the expiry of the limitation period is rather more difficult than to amend prior to the expiry of the limitation period; see the notes in the *White Book* at para 20/5–8/7.

 (ii) a complexity of building contract matters (and their comparative unfamiliarity to many general practitioners) results in many cases in delay in their prosecution. In *Renown Investments (Holdings) Ltd* v *F Shepherd & Son* (1976) 120 SJ 840 it was established that that complexity did not of itself render plaintiffs immune from the danger of being struck out for want of prosecution. ie *Birkett* v *James* [1977] 3 WLR 38 has rendered it very difficult indeed successfully to strike out an action for want of prosecution prior to the expiry of the limitation period, but after that time the plaintiff is vulnerable to such an application and in building contract matters the success rate of those applications is unusually high (see p 143).

Where a complex matter is nearing the expiration of the limitation period, these two factors may encourage a plaintiff to choose arbitration and a defendant to choose litigation in the court. An arbitrator does have power to disallow amendments (*Creighton* v *Law Car Insurance Co* [1910] 2 KB 738), but it is a brave arbitrator who will do so. More importantly, the House of Lords has now decided that arbitrations may continue notwithstanding inordinate and inexcusable delay by a claimant, and claimants are accordingly now in the fortunate position of not having to concern themselves unduly about the danger of losing their claims through want of prosecution (*Bremer Vulkan* v *South India Shipping* [1981] 2 All ER 289).

6 Commercial considerations

Arbitration is by its nature less aggressive than High Court proceedings. In the minds of many commercial men the service of a High Court writ represents something tantamount to a declaration of war and arbitration is frequently seen as far more in keeping with the commercial image of many business organisations.

Where a claimant has in mind the possibility of further contracts with a respondent but nonetheless wishes to pursue a particular dispute, then that can be an overwhelming consideration which would cause that party to choose arbitration rather than High Court litigation.

7 Privacy

Parties to building contract litigation are sometimes keen to keep the litigation out of the courts because they are sensitive to the possibility of publicity. On other occasions they may feel that their opponent is sensitive to publicity and regard this as a good reason to keep the matter in the court.

The distinction between court proceedings and arbitration in terms of the privacy they afford to the litigants is probably exaggerated in many cases. Although the theory of the matter is that trials in the High Court are open to the public, in practice it is rare for a building contract trial in the Official Referees corridor to attract any publicity at all. Where the trial is in one of the courtrooms near to the main hall in the Royal Courts of Justice there may be the occasional group of bemused tourists who 'look in' for a few minutes before wandering off in search of something more interesting. In reality, the supposed advantage of arbitration proceedings to a sensitive party is often illusory in building contract cases. If a party does suffer from publication of its affairs it is very frequently as a result of gossip in the construction industry and the City and that gossip will do no more or less than in arbitration proceedings. That said, parties are sometimes nervous of court proceedings where the subject-matter is sensitive and this nervousness of itself is sometimes successfully exploited by the other party.

8 International element

In the case of international contracts, particularly contracts with foreign governments or bodies sponsored by foreign governments, very different considerations apply. Where the parties to a contract are in different countries each is unlikely to want any disputes resolved on the home territory of the other. It is plainly a great advantage in many respects to be able to fight on one's home ground. Further, foreign governments are frequently most reluctant to submit to the jurisdiction of the court of any other country as it is an affront to their dignity.

For these reasons, arbitration agreements in contracts with an international element are of particular importance. They frequently provide that disputes should be settled under the Rules of Conciliation and Arbitration of the International Chamber of Commerce (the ICC). The standard form of building contract most widely used for international building contracts, the FIDC contract, contains such an arbitration clause.

Where court proceedings are commenced despite a domestic arbitration agreement, the other party *may* apply to the court under the Arbitration Act 1950, s 4, and the court *may* order a stay of the court proceedings pending the arbitration. The court has a discretion as to whether the matter should go to arbitration. Where, however, a party issues proceedings and there is a 'non-domestic' arbitration agreement within the meaning of the Arbitration Act 1975, s 1, then the other party *may* apply to the court under this 1975 Act and the court *must* then stay the court proceedings. It has no discretion.

From the point of view of an English claimant, litigation in the court is very likely to be preferable to arbitration under the rules of the ICC. In the English courts he would have a natural advantage over an overseas opponent. See p 154 for a description of the ICC Court of Arbitration.

9 Insolvency and impecuniosity

Legal aid is not available for arbitration, and if a party is within the financial limits for legal aid then that may be a conclusive reason for him preferring the court, whether he be plaintiff or defendant. Likewise, because it is extremely difficult for an unassisted party to obtain an order for the payment of costs where his opponent is an assisted party (see the Legal Aid Act 1974, s 13) a party whose opponent is or may be within the financial limits is more likely to prefer arbitration, where s 13 has no application.

As to the legal aid consideration in section 4 summonses, it was held in *Smith* v *Pearl Assurance Co* [1939] 1 All ER 95 that the poverty of a litigant is not a ground for keeping the dispute in the court. In *Fakes* v *Taylor Woodrow Construction Ltd* [1973] 1 QB 436, however, the plaintiff showed that his poverty was caused by the defendant itself and he was accordingly entitled to keep the dispute in the court where legal aid was available to him.

If a party is in danger of becoming insolvent then that is a matter which is likely to encourage him towards arbitration and his opponent towards litigation in the court. The High Court exercises control over arbitrations in respect of such matters as security for costs, preservation of property and appointment of receivers under the Arbitration Act 1950, s 12(6), but these remedies are more conveniently available where the whole action is in the High Court, and in any event the High Court probably takes a more robust view than do arbitrators of the effect of potential insolvency of one of the parties.

10 Technical complexity

It is rare for building contract disputes to contain points of such technical complexity that they are beyond the wit of a High Court judge or Official Referee. There are, however, recurring building problems (in particular those relating to the design of foundations, the frames of buildings and condensation) where the technical issues are, to say the least, difficult and where an arbitrator may be better able to understand the issues fully. That can be a consideration to lean a party in favour of arbitration.

Technical complexity should not be confused with understanding of building contract practices and quantity surveying practices. These issues tend in the end to be legal issues and the Official Referees are familiar with the practice of the building industry.

11 Pleadings and evidence

Parties sometimes wish to have their dispute dealt with in arbitration because they imagine that this will obviate the need to prepare lengthy and unnecessary pleadings. In fact, pleadings in arbitrations tend to be little different from pleadings in High Court litigation. Arbitrators normally make orders at the preliminary meeting for delivery of points of claim, points of defence and counterclaim and points of reply and defence to counterclaim which correspond more or less with the time scale one would expect in the High Court. The arbitrator may make further directions for the delivery of submissions or contentions; the terminology does not matter greatly and all these documents are in the nature of pleadings in the sense generally understood in High Court litigation.

There is an implied provision in arbitration agreements under the

Arbitration Act 1950, s 12(1), that the parties are deemed to have agreed to 'do all other things which the proceedings on the reference to the arbitrator or umpire may require'; and this provision is construed to authorise an arbitrator to direct delivery of pleadings and exercise his discretion as to allowing or disallowing amendment of these (*Edward Lloyd Ltd* v *Sturgeon Falls & Co* (1901) 85 LT 162; *Creighton* v *Law Car etc Insurance Co* (1910) 2 KB 738). Despite this, an arbitrator probably does have more flexibility than the High Court with regard to pleadings and where a party already has the benefit of a 'non-legal' but carefully researched and lengthy claim document it may be easier for that party to use the claim document with comparatively little amendment in an arbitration.

As far as evidence is concerned, the difference between arbitration and High Court litigation is principally procedural. The Arbitration Act 1950, s 12, contains provision for parties to the arbitration (s 12(1)) and other witnesses (s 12(2)) to give evidence on oath. If necessary that evidence can be bought pursuant to a writ of subpoena ad testificandum (s 12(4)) and the court has further wide powers under s 12(6). It seems that perjury committed in an arbitration is tantamount to perjury at common law and punishable as such (*R* v *Crossley* (1909) 100 LT 463 CA).

Accordingly, evidence will only rarely be a consideration which will influence the choice between arbitration and litigation in the High Court.

12 Discovery of documents

It is normal for the discovery process in arbitration to be conducted in much the same way as in the High Court. It is provided in the Arbitration Act 1950, s 12(1):

'Unless a contrary expression is expressed therein, every arbitration agreement shall, where such a provision is applicable to the reference, be deemed to contain a provision that the parties to the reference, and all persons claiming through them respectively, shall, subject to any legal objection, submit to ... produce before the arbitrator or umpire all documents within their possession or power respectively which may be required or called for, and do all other things which during the proceedings on the reference the arbitrator or umpire may require.'

There is further provision in s 12(4) which provides that any party to a reference under an arbitration agreement may sue out a writ of subpoena duces tecum (but not so as to compel any person to produce any document which he could not be compelled to produce on the trial of an action in the court); and there is a further general power under s 12(6) for the High Court to make orders in respect of discovery of documents.

The significant difference between arbitration and High Court litigation as regards discovery is, accordingly, as to enforcement only. It is the common practice of arbitrators to make original orders in respect of discovery in exactly the same way as in the High Court and the form of the list of documents is normally the same. However, if a party wishes to enforce a discovery order he does so by issuing an originating summons in the High Court either pursuant to the Arbitration Act 1950, s12(6)(b) or pursuant to the Arbitration Act 1979, s 5(1). The jurisdiction conferred on the High Court may be exercised by a judge in chambers or Master or Admiralty Registrar (Ord 73, r 3); in practice in building contract matters the originating summons is normally taken out in the Queen's Bench Division before a Master.

Accordingly, discovery is not generally a major consideration in the choice between arbitration or litigation in the High Court, but if severe problems are expected at discovery it marginally assists to have the action heard in the High Court.

13 Can the substantive law be different?

The general rule was stated in *David Taylor & Son Ltd* v *Barnett Trading Co* [1953] 1 WLR 562,568:

> 'The duty of an arbitrator is to decide the questions submitted to him according to the legal rights of the parties, and not according to what he may consider fair and reasonable under all the circumstances.'

That is the theory. In practice, arbitrators frequently are heavily influenced by what they see as a just solution, and that vision of justice may differ from that of the High Court.

There may well be occasions where an arbitrator departs from the law; certainly arbitrators are less likely than the High Court to be convinced by complex legal arguments which might apparently fly in the face of what seems to be common sense on the particular facts.

In respect of arbitration commenced after 1 August 1979 the appeals procedure in the Arbitration Act 1950, s 21, has been replaced by the procedure in the Arbitration Act 1979, s 1. Under the 1979 Act appeal lies to the High Court on any question of law arising out of an award made on an arbitration agreement (s 1(2)), and the Court may require the arbitrator to state the reasons for his award in sufficient detail to enable the Court to consider the question of law (s 1(5)). It is, however, necessary for one of the parties to give notice to the arbitrator concerned that a reasoned order would be required *before* the award was made (s 1(6)).

14 Getting into the right forum

Having made a decision as to whether it is better to be in arbitration or in the court, how is a party to have his dispute heard in that forum? This question is considered below.

(a) A plaintiff who prefers the court

If it is comfortably less than six years since the date of the contract, the plaintiff should simply issue a writ and proceed in the court. As soon as the defendant takes a step in the action (see p 111), the litigation is firmly established in the courts. Some plaintiffs attempt to force the defendant into taking a step in the action as soon as possible (eg by refusing to grant an extension of time, however short) in the hope that the defendant will lose the opportunity of arbitration before having a chance to consider it fully. A plaintiff will sometimes delay issuing his Ord 14 summons until after the defence is due specifically with this point in mind.

If the defendant does serve a section 4 summons then the plaintiff must oppose it as best he can. Where the plaintiff has reason to believe that the defendant will successfully take out a section 4 summons, then that is an especially good reason for the plaintiff to take out an Ord 14 summons in respect of as much of the claim as he can since that part of the claim will be immune from the stay to arbitration (*Ellis Mechanical Services Ltd* v *Wates Construction Ltd* (1976) 2 BLR 57).

If six years have passed since the date of the formation of the contract (or will have passed by the time the defendant is forced to take a step in the action) there may be a limitation risk, and if the contract contains an arbitration clause the plaintiff would be well advised to serve a protective arbitration notice. It is possible for such a notice to be drafted making it quite plain that the plaintiff regards the High Court as the proper forum for the dispute (see p 148); and, although the notice will protect the position for the purpose of limitation in a subsequent arbitration it will not of itself operate actually to put any arbitration into being.

If the defendant himself serves an arbitration notice, the plaintiff can simply ignore it and proceed with the High Court action unless and until prevented from doing so by an order under the Arbitration Act 1950, s 4, or, in the case of a non-domestic arbitration agreement, under the Arbitration Act 1975, s 1.

(b) A plaintiff who prefers arbitration

Unless there is a limitation risk, the claimant first serves a notice requiring the respondent to concur in the appointment of an arbitrator. This will protect him for the purposes of limitation

(Limitation Act 1980, s 34). If the respondent responds to the notice and it is possible to agree upon who should be the arbitrator, the claimant approaches the agreed arbitrator with a view to persuading the arbitrator to accept the appointment as rapidly as possible. If it is not possible to agree upon an arbitrator, generally the arbitration clause provides that the arbitrator shall be appointed by the president for the time being of the RIBA or sometimes the RICS (or similar body). The claimant requests such a nomination and then approaches the nominated person with a view to persuading him to accept the reference as soon as possible. In certain cases the court has power to appoint an arbitrator (Arbitration Act 1950, s 10, as amended by the Arbitration Act 1979, s 6(3)).

The arbitration does not commence until an arbitrator has been appointed and has accepted the appointment.

Where there is or may be a limitation risk a cautious claimant will often regard it as desirable also to issue but not serve a writ in the High Court. It is possible for the court to restrain an arbitration by injunction in exceptional circumstances and to revoke the authority of the arbitrator where the arbitrator is or may be partial (Arbitration Act 1950, s 24(1)) or the arbitration involves a question of fraud (Arbitration Act 1950, s 24(2)), or where the arbitrator is guilty of misconduct (Arbitration Act 1950, s 23(1), or where the arbitrator himself fails to use all reasonable dispatch (Arbitration Act 1950, s 13(3)). Where an arbitrator is removed or his authority is revoked, then the court has power under the Arbitration Act 1950, s 25, to appoint an alternative arbitrator, but it also has power if it thinks fit to order that the arbitration agreement shall cease to have effect with respect to the dispute referred. A claimant will, therefore, be better protected in cases of limitation risk where he has a High Court writ upon file in the court. Unless renewed the writ will only remain valid for twelve months beginning with the date of its issue (Ord 6, r 8(1)), and accordingly it is counter-productive in the circumstances to issue the protective writ before there is any limitation risk.

(c) A respondent who prefers the court

Once an arbitration has commenced it may be very difficult for the respondent to resist the matter proceeding by arbitration. He may be able to apply to the court if the dispute is or may be outside the terms of the arbitration agreement; the High Court will restrain an arbitration in certain circumstances (see the cases cited in Part 2 of the *White Book* at para 3733); and 'if one thing is quite plain, it is that an arbitrator cannot give himself jurisdiction by deciding in his favour some preliminary point upon which his jurisdiction depends'

(*Smith* v *Martin* [1925] 1 KB 745). However, the grounds upon which the court will restrain an arbitration by injunction are limited and a party who wishes to have the dispute heard in the court will usually have a far better chance of fulfilling that wish if he fights upon the ground of a section 4 summons. Accordingly, the defending party will in many cases be well advised to issue a writ prior to the appointment of an arbitrator (and if necessary in the short intervening period between notice to concur in the appointment of an arbitrator, and the actual appointment of an arbitrator).

If the party who wishes litigation in the court has a money claim, then a writ with statement of claim indorsed may be issued and served claiming that sum. It is immaterial that it may be met by a far greater counterclaim. If the defending party does not have any money claim at all, he can nonetheless issue a writ claiming a declaratory judgment that he is not liable to meet the other's claim. The Rules of the Supreme Court, Ord 15, r 16, provides:

'No action or other proceedings shall be open to objection on the ground that a merely declaratory judgment or order is sought thereby, and the Court may make binding declarations of right whether or not any consequential relief is or could be claimed.'

An application for a declaratory judgment should not be made prematurely since the person against whom no claim has been made may not obtain a declaration that no such claim exists (*Re Clay* [1919] 1 Ch 66 CA).

In such circumstances, the defendant to the declaratory writ (ie the party who has the major claim) is very likely to issue a section 4 summons. However, the plaintiff will be entitled to all the arguments normally available on a section 4 summons and of particular importance in building contract matters is the effect of *Taunton-Collins* v *Crombie* [1964] 1 WLR 63 CA (see p 115), where a stay was refused because there were more than two parties.

It would be unusual for an arbitrator to accept an appointment in a case where he knew that a High Court writ had been issued and served and was being actively pursued. The plaintiff in the High Court proceedings (ie the potential respondent in the arbitration) should accordingly put any proposed arbitrator on notice of the position, and in any extreme case where a proposed arbitrator threatens to try to shortcut the section 4 procedure the plaintiff should carefully consider the possibility of obtaining an injunction restraining the prospective arbitrator.

(d) A defendant who prefers arbitration

A party who is potentially a respondent to an arbitration is sometimes well advised to commence the arbitration himself and so become a claimant. There are two reasons for this.

First, a claimant in an arbitration has marginally more control over the proceedings than a respondent. In particular, a claimant can often dictate the pace of the arbitration proceedings more effectively than a respondent.

The second reason is that once he has obtained the appointment of an arbitrator he has substantially closed the door to an opponent who would prefer the High Court. Usually, the only prospect such an opponent will have will be to move quickly and issue proceedings prior to the appointment of the arbitrator.

If a plaintiff has issued and served a writ, a defendant who prefers arbitration must before taking any step in the proceedings, issue a summons either under the Arbitration Act 1950, s 4, or under the Arbitration Act 1975, s 1, depending upon whether the arbitration agreement is a domestic arbitration agreement within the meaning of the Arbitration Act 1975, s 1.

Chapter 8
Litigation in the High Court

In principle, building contract litigation is like other litigation at common law. In the High Court, it is properly commenced in the Queen's Bench Division and the Rules of the Supreme Court apply. In practice, it tends to differ in certain material respects. In particular:

(i) Very frequently building contract disputes involve a multiplicity of issues. The pleadings often involve lengthy tabulations and calculations concerning the cost of building works which the lawyers are not usually in a position to evaluate without the assistance of experts. The contracts are often long and complicated and can give rise to as many legal points as the parties choose to identify; but within the complexities there are often undeniable truths that can be made to stand out.

(ii) Almost all building contract litigation, if it goes to trial, is tried before the Official Referee. The Official Referee's Court is in fact most sensible and helpful but it is unfamiliar to many lawyers.

(iii) The Official Referee's Court is, in effect, a specialist court for building contract litigation. There is also a specialist building contract bar, and there are firms of solicitors that specialise in building contract law. The existence of these specialists can create a hostile environment for the unequipped stranger.

The fountain of most knowledge of High Court procedure is the Supreme Court Practice, commonly known as the *White Book*. The *White Book* is published in two volumes every three years (the current edition is the 1979 edition) and a cumulative supplement is released every few months.

Volume 1 of the *White Book* contains not only the Rules of the Supreme Court but also lengthy and very useful commentaries. The Rules themselves have the force of statute in matters of procedure, being made under the Judicature Act 1925 and other statutes. The notes, which are printed in slightly smaller type, do not have any formal force of law, but they do provide very useful cross references and guidance and are taken to have a persuasive value.

Volume 2 of the *White Book* contains Parts 2 – 7. Of particular use are Part 2 (which contains the general forms prescribed by the Rules and the Queen's Bench Masters' practice forms, which also ought to be followed,), Part 4A (which reproduces the Masters' practice directions), Part 4E (which consists of a timetable showing when different steps require to be taken under the rules), and Part 9B (which contains inter alia the Arbitration Acts with notes).

For those unfamiliar with the *White Book* it can be a daunting work. The following comments may be helpful:

1 It is desirable to read the rules before reading the notes. It is often convenient to look at the contents page to see which is the relevant order before looking at the index.

2 The index to the *White Book* is to be found at the end of Volume 1 and is an acquired taste. It is worthwhile noting that there are three sorts of reference in the index:

—References with only one oblique (eg 14/1) are references to a rule itself (for example, Ord 14 r 1 appears at paragraph 14/1.

—References with two obliques (eg 14/1/1) are references to notes (for example, para 14/1/1 is the first of the 5 notes which appear to Ord 14, r 1, itself.

—References in square brackets are references to paragraph numbers in Volume 2.

3 When looking at any particular rule, it is often useful to glance through at least the headings of all the other rules in that particular order.

4 It is often difficult when looking at precedent books of court forms to distinguish between what is required by the rules, and what is suggested by the editor of such books. Part 2 in Volume 2 of the *White Book* contains all the forms which it is *necessary* to follow.

5 The cumulative supplements become of special importance towards the end of the three-year life span of each edition. It is useful to mark in the main work the passages revised in the supplements.

6 The function of the court is, or ought to be, to assist the parties in the matter of formal requirements. Where possible, the court officials at the Central Office of the High Court in the Strand are usually prepared to give advice as to formal requirements over the telephone (the telephone number of the Central Office is 01-405 7641). Alternatively; there is sitting every working day a Practice Master who will not only give guidance as to procedural matters upon personal application but has power to make orders and directions if appropriate. It is, however, the case that both Masters and

the court officials are sometimes terse in the giving of advice to solicitors upon matters which the solicitors might reasonably be expected to look up for themselves.

In the Queen's Bench Division, hearings are either in open court or in chambers. In building contract cases, practically all hearings are in chambers except the trial itself. The general rule is that a Master has power to sit in every application in chambers (Ord 32, r 11) although there are some exceptions given in the notes to that rule. Solicitors have rights of audience in proceedings in chambers, and so do their legal executives and managing and other responsible clerks (*Vimbos* v *Meadowcroft* (1902) 46 SJ 2). Neither counsel nor solicitors appear robed at proceedings in chambers.

The substantial majority of building contract cases are settled. Indeed, the view is often expressed that the trial of a building contract case is of itself an indication of the failure of the legal advisers of one or both parties. In practice, the terms of settlement are usually very heavily influenced by the result of interlocutory hearings in chambers, and it is usually unreasonable for a solicitor to expect general common law barristers to be able to match the advice of specialist barristers.

Particular aspects of building contract litigation in the High Court are considered elsewhere in this book. Some of the more important features are summarised below.

It is a mistake to assume that a party is bound to accept his opponent's choice to go to arbitration, even if the contract contains an arbitration clause. If a claimant serves an arbitration notice it may be possible for the other party to get the dispute before the courts by issuing a writ, and if the plaintiff sues in the court it may be possible for the defendant to obtain a stay of proceedings under the Arbitration Act 1950, s 4. See p 108.

It is often a mistake to assume that an 'expert' will be able to deal with all of the detailed facts, especially where those facts relate to the valuation of work. Surveyors, and particularly quantity surveyors, provide an invaluable service to the building industry by adopting pragmatic attitudes to complex matters but they are not lawyers and many of their most adamant assertions will wilt under the judicial gaze. The parties' lawyers should check the legal basis of the expert's figures, particularly where terms like 'preliminaries', 'claims' or 'contras' are used.

Order 14 is of especial importance in building contract cases, even where they involve a mass of detail. There may be a legal argument that renders the detail irrelevant. Remember:

(i)   it is common practice to argue points of law at Ord 14 if the relevant facts are not in dispute.

(ii) even if the assigned Queen's Bench Division Master will not give judgment under Ord 14, an Official Referee might.

(iii) an Ord 14 judgment for part of a claim represents a major psychological advantage for the remaining part of the litigation, which may be drawn out and complex.

(iv) a summons issued by a defendant for a stay of court proceedings under the Arbitration Act 1950, s 4, is of itself no sufficient answer to an Ord 14 summons. The practice of the court is to enter judgment for the sum it considers to be indisputably due and to refer the balance of the dispute (if any) to arbitration. See p 113

(v) an application for interim payment under Ord 29, Pt II, may be made in tandem with or instead of an Ord 14 application.

It is sometimes thought that the interlocutory proceedings of litigation are merely formal, and that the court will be able to do justice at trial. This is frequently a mistake. Even if a case is not settled before trial, the conduct of the interlocutory stages will usually have caused one party materially to improve his position, and may have practically guaranteed him a judgment which he could not possibly have relied upon at the outset of proceedings.

The plaintiff begins by issuing a writ. Sometimes the statement of claim is endorsed on the writ or served with it; on other occasions it may be up to a year before the statement of claim is served.

If the writ is issued out of a district registry there may be a skirmish as to whether the action be tried in the district registry or in the central office in London. The rules as to whether or not an action is transferred from a district registry to London have recently been revised following the abolition of the appearance but the issue of transfer to London remains the first of the areas for interlocutory dispute.

Once the statement of claim has been served then it is common for the plaintiff to take out an Ord 14 summons or for the defendant to take out a section 4 summons. If one or both of these summonses is opposed and goes to special appointment it can often take six months or more for both summonses to be disposed of.

The parties then resume the process of pleadings. Commonly, the statement of claim is followed by a defence and counterclaim which is in turn followed by the plaintiff's reply and defence to counterclaim. In theory, these pleadings ought to follow within fourteen days of each other (Ord 18, rr 2 and 3) but in practice this time is almost never sufficient in a building case, and time for the service of pleadings is extended by consent or pursuant to the issue of a time summons under Ord 3, r 5. In practice, the time to close of pleadings in building contract cases in the High Court is more usually counted in months than in weeks.

There is a provision in Ord 24, r 2, requiring the parties to give discovery within fourteen days after the close of pleadings, but this rule is honoured more in the breach than in the observance. In fact, there is very often a period of procedural limbo after the pleadings have closed until the plaintiff eventually takes out a summons for directions under Ord 25, r 1. Very frequently, the master hearing that summons simply orders a transfer to the Official Referee; in theory the order is made upon the application of a party (Ord 36, r 1) but the Masters of the Queen's Bench Division are not slow to encourage the parties to make that application and it is very rare for a proper case not to be transferred to the Official Referee. The plaintiff's solicitor is responsible for effecting the transfer, and the case will be assigned to one of the three Official Referees. There is then a further summons before that Referee and directions are usually given on the spot. The directions usually set out a timetable for all the remaining steps. A trial date is usually fixed on the spot typically some nine months or more hence.

In many cases, there are further summonses before trial often based upon failure or alleged failure of one or other party to give proper discovery or to give particulars in the form requested or ordered by the Official Referee. It is comparatively rare for the parties to fail to settle before trial.

It is misleading to regard building contract litigation as following pre-ordained steps. To adopt a 'check list' approach can be particularly disastrous and lead to great delay and expense. Skilfully conducted, the litigation is in some respects like a game of chess. Each party tries to take the initiative where it can, and is constantly adjusting its position in the light of the other party's position. During the proceedings, the confidence of one party usually grows at the expense of the confidence of the other. It becomes clear who is likely to win and the parties settle. Sometimes, a party can achieve an overwhelming advantage quite early, at the Ord 14 stage for example. Sometimes, he gradually builds up an advantage, and by continually seeking particulars and admissions he at last persuades his opponent that the latter is not going to be able to put up a good enough case.

There are some sorts of litigation, such as actions by landlords for possession of premises, where it is at trial that the action is won or lost. It is rare for the trial of a building contract case to represent an attractive prospect for either party. Ordinarily, the underlying purpose of each step in the litigation is to force the other party into a mood for settlement on the right terms.

Chapter 9
Order 14

Order 14 entitles the court to award summary judgment without trial, and is the only one which is widely known by its number. Rule 1 provides as follows:

> '1—(1) Where in an action to which this rule applies a statement of claim has been served on a defendant and that defendant has given notice of intention to defend the action, the Plaintiff may, on the ground that that Defendant has no defence to a claim included in the Writ, or to a particular part of such a claim, or has no defence to such a claim or part except as to the amount of any damages claimed, apply to the Court for judgment against that Defendant.'

The words 'given notice of intention to defend the action' were substituted for the previous words 'entered an Appearance in the action' by the RSC (Writ and Appearance) 1979 (SI 1979 No 1716). The defendant gives notice of his intention to defend the action, if he so wishes, in the form of Acknowledgement of Service.

The raison d'être of Ord 14 is clear. Where a plaintiff has a claim to which the defendant has no defence worthy of the name it would be manifestly unjust if the plaintiff were put to the expense and delay of further pleadings, discovery and inspection of documents, taking out a summons for directions, setting the action down for trial, obtaining a trial date and trial itself. The purpose of these procedures is to do justice between parties in genuine dispute and not to allow a debtor the right to delay or even avoid altogether his obligation to pay his debts. Indeed, it is frequently said that it is a major defect of the County Court Rules that they do not have any provision similar to Ord 14 in the High Court, and it is frequently this consideration that causes plaintiffs to commence proceedings in the High Court rather than in the county court even where their claims are within the financial limits of the county court jurisdiction.

Unlike in some other jurisdictions, the High Court in England and Wales does not automatically consider whether the plaintiff is entitled to summary judgment; if a plaintiff wishes to obtain summary judgment he must issue an Ord 14 summons and this places upon the plaintiff's legal advisers a special obligation to consider whether or not the claim is within the scope of Ord 14. The failure of those advisers to have regard to Ord 14 can cause a plaintiff great damage, and indeed in a clear case might amount to actionable negligence.

In building contract cases, where trial in the courts or arbitration can be long delayed and expensive, Ord 14 has even more importance than in many other areas of the law, particularly in the case of claims by contractors who spend a great deal of money in the execution of the works and need prompt payment if they are to survive. The courts, in exercising their jurisdiction under Ord 14, recognise this special feature of building contract litigation and arbitration, and accordingly are prepared to adopt in building contract cases a more robust approach than in other sorts of case. As Lawton LJ said in *Ellis Mechanical Services Ltd* v *Wates Construction Limited* (1976) 2 BLR 57:

> 'The Courts are aware of what happens in these building disputes; cases go either to arbitration or before an Official Referee; they drag on and on and on; the cash flow is held up. In the majority of cases, because one party or the other cannot wait any longer for the money, there is some kind of compromise, very often not based on the justice of the case but on the financial situation of one of the parties. That sort of result is to be avoided if possible. In my judgment it can be avoided if the Court makes a robust approach, as the Master did in this case, to the jurisdiction under Order 14.'

Now that the court has power to order interim payment under Ord 29, Pt II, it is possible that it will adopt an equally robust (or even a more robust) approach under Ord 29; see p 106. Much of what follows in this chapter applies as much to Ord 29, Pt II, as to Ord 14; the applications will ordinarily be made together and will probably be seen, in practice, as a single application upon alternative grounds.

Of course, not all cases are suitable for Ord 14, but the decision as to whether or not to proceed by Ord 14 is frequently the most important tactical decision to be made by a plaintiff in building contract litigation. If the case is suitable for Ord 14, then this can carry with it several advantages.

First, a judgment under Ord 14 can be obtained very much more quickly than a judgment at trial. The full course of litigation in the courts or arbitration can and frequently does run to two or three years. It is usually possible to obtain an effective Ord 14 hearing within about six months from the date of the issue of the writ. Even if the defendant appeals against a Master's Order for Judgment, then an appeal before a judge can usually be heard fairly quickly.

Secondly, the costs of Ord 14 are usually but a fraction of the costs of trial.

These advantages are fairly self-evident. There are other advantages of Ord 14 for a plaintiff that are less widely recognised. In particular, Ord 14 can be an effective way of bringing the minds of the defendant and his advisers to bear upon the issues of the litigation. It is very common for defendants to put from their minds in the early stages of litigation precisely how they will defend a claim. Although pleadings are intended to set out the issues they all too often represent nothing more than a catalogue of assertions and points of law that might or might not avail the party putting them forward. Once they are served, the pleadings are often ignored by the parties until trial itself, when the parties finally decide how to present their respective cases. Different considerations apply to the defendant's affidavit to show cause against an Ord 14 application. It is not sufficient for the defendant to deny the debt generally (*Wallingford* v *Mutual Society* (1880) 5 App Cas 685). A defendant who raises transparently spurious matters in his defence at Ord 14 will merely irritate the court and increase the chances of a judgment being given against him. The realism induced in a defendant's mind by an Ord 14 application can not only discourage him from subsequently raising spurious matters in his defence but can also force him to consider more carefully whether or not he ought to make an early realistic offer of settlement.

These considerations can sometimes be sufficient to make an Ord 14 application attractive to a plaintiff in circumstances where there is only an outside prospect of the plaintiff being awarded a substantial judgment under Ord 14. The limiting factor is often the plaintiff's ability to swear properly the necessary affidavit; see p 95.

In broad terms, the factors influencing the decision whether or not to make an Ord 14 application are the same whether the contract in question contains an arbitration clause or not. Generally, where a claim or a part of a claim is within the scope of Ord 14, then the court will give judgment under Ord 14 and refer the balance of the dispute, if any, to arbitration (*Ellis Mechanical Services Ltd* v *Wates Construction* (1976) 2 BLR 57). It appears that this is a practical distinction between the powers of the court under Ord 14, and the powers of the court to order interim payment under Ord 29, Pt II, since it seems unlikely that the courts will order interim payment in a case destined for arbitration. Order 14 can sometimes have a particular attraction for plaintiffs where there is an arbitration clause if the plaintiffs would benefit from some point of law being put before the court rather than before an arbitrator without legal qualifications.

The court may give an Ord 14 judgment for a part only of the plaintiff's claim; and if there is a part of the plaintiff's claim that is within the scope of Ord 14, then it is usually in the plaintiff's interest to seek an Ord 14 judgment (coupled, perhaps, with an application for interim payment under Ord 29, Pt II) in respect of that part, even if it is a comparatively minor part of his total claim. This not only accelerates the time when the plaintiff can receive some of his money but also often represents a major tactical advantage. In an area of law where the rate of settlement is so high it is extremely important for the plaintiff to try to sap the enthusiasm and confidence of the defendant as quickly as possible. A defendant will often resist an Ord 14 summons for a minor part of the claim without any real thought, as though this were a reflex reaction. If such a defendant loses an early skirmish at Ord 14 he will often form a less sanguine view of his overall prospects.

In cases which are inevitably destined for the Official Referee's Court, especially cases which are destined to be effectively re-pleaded in a Scott Schedule, Ord 14 summonses are sometimes issued as a means of accelerating the proceedings. In such cases the procedure in the ordinary course of events is often as follows:

(1) The plaintiff issues a writ and serves a statement of claim;
(2) The defendant returns the acknowledgement of service showing an intention to defend the proceedings;
(3) The defendant obtains an extension of time for service of his defence;
(4) The defendant obtains a further extension of time for service of his defence;
(5) The defendant takes out a time summons for service of his defence;
(6) The defendant takes out a further time summons for service of his defence;
(7) The defendant serves his defence and counterclaim;
(8) The plaintiff serves his reply and defence to counterclaim;
(9) The parties fail to give automatic discovery;
(10) The plaintiff issues a summons for directions; and
(11) The Master makes an Order at the hearing of the summons for directions for transfer to the Official Referee.

This process is sometimes truncated, as follows:

(1) The plaintiff issues a writ and serves a statement of claim;
(2) The defendant returns the acknowledgement of service showing an intention to defend the proceedings;
(3) The plaintiff issues an Ord 14 summons returnable in the 10.30 list, and serves an affidavit in support;
(4) The defendant serves an affidavit in reply;
(5) The Master makes an Order on the hearing of the Ord 14 summons for transfer to the Official Referee.

Solicitors are under a special duty in this regard resulting from their duties not only to their clients but also to the court. In *Marsh* v *Joseph* [1897] 1 Ch 213, 245 it was said:

> 'Where negligence or other breach of duty is committed by a solicitor, an officer of the Court, in a matter of which the Court has seisin, the Court may, and, if it can do full justice, will summarily order its officer to make good the loss occasioned by his neglect or breach of duty.'

In practice, it is frequently this duty, and not any material disadvantage, that prevents the issue of Ord 14 summonses. It remains to be seen whether and to what extent a plaintiff will be able to circumnavigate this obstacle by making his application, not for judgment under Ord 14, but for interim payment under the new provisions of Ord 29, Pt II.

In an inappropriate case, an application under Ord 14 can of course retard the plaintiff's position. It is, however, probably true that it is more common for a plaintiff to fail to make an Ord 14 application when he should than it is for a plaintiff to make an Ord 14 application when he should not.

1 No defence

Order 14, r 1, prescribes the ground upon which the plaintiff may apply to the court for summary judgment, namely that 'that defendant has no defence to a claim included in the Writ, or to a particular part of such claim, or has no defence to such claim or part except as to the amount of any damages claimed'. Further, the application must be supported by an affidavit verifying the facts upon which the claim, or the part of the claim, to which the application relates is based and stating that in the deponent's belief there is no defence to that claim or part, as the case may be, or no defence as to the amount of any damages claimed (Ord 14, r 2).

It seems that the test as to whether there is a defence is objective for the purposes of Ord 14, r 1; and that the test of whether there is a defence for the purposes of Ord 14, r 2, is a subjective one (ie does the plaintiff believe that there is no defence?) That subjective test, however, only goes to the question of whether it is proper for the plaintiff to swear his affidavit in support in the required form. For the purpose of determining whether or not the Ord 14 application is a proper one, the court will decide not whether the plaintiff believes there is a defence nor whether the defendant believes there is a defence but whether there is in fact a defence. The court must decide this without trying whatever matter the defendant seeks to put forward by way of defence, and accordingly the word 'defence' has been construed as meaning 'bona fide defence' or 'fairly arguable defence' or 'reasonable ground of defence' or 'good defence on the merits'.

In theory, it is only half the battle at Ord 14 for the plaintiff to show that the defendant has no defence. Ord 14, r 3, envisages that the defendant might satisfy the court that there is an issue or question in dispute which ought to be tried or that there ought for some other reason to be a trial of the claim or part of the claim. Ord 14, r 4, permits a defendant to 'show cause against an application under r1'. In practical terms, r 3 and r 4 add little in commercial building contract cases to the 'no defence' test save to strengthen the element of discretion inevitably present at Ord 14 hearings. The court operates a single test: is it abundantly plain from the evidence on affidavit that the defendant is going to lose and is merely playing for time or being hopelessly optimistic about his prospects at trial?

The degree of proof required from the plaintiff varies from case to case. In the case of a claim by a contractor for payment, the certificate of the architect that the sum claimed is due is usually regarded as very cogent evidence, and is generally sufficient unless the defendant is able to put forward a bona fide set-off or counterclaim. Where there is no certificate, the court will usually accept the contractor's valuation of work done unless the defendant can show that there are good grounds to suggest that the claim is, in fact, excessive. In the absence of something convincing from the defendant, the court does not require a plaintiff contractor to adduce expert evidence as to the reasonableness of the sum claimed. In the case of a claim by an employer for delay, the court is likely to require a certificate given pursuant to the terms of the contract and in the absence of such certificate will not require much convincing by the contractor that the question of responsibility for the delay ought to go to trial. In the case of a claim by an employer for defective work, the plaintiff will usually have a much more difficult task at Ord 14 and will have to show both that the work is defective and that it is the contractor that is responsible. It will be cogent evidence of the former that the plaintiff has incurred the expense of having the work done again, and the court is not usually impressed by a defects claim if the plaintiff is using the works for their intended purpose without showing any intention to rectify them. If the court is satisfied that there are defects, it will often assume that the contractor is responsible for them unless the contractor can show that they are or may be the responsibility of some other person such as the architect.

The courts look at the surrounding circumstances if they appear from the affidavit evidence. Where, for example, a contractor does work for an employer it sometimes happens that the employer makes no payment at all and raises no complaint as to the work until he makes his affidavit in reply to an Ord 14 summons, where he alleges defects to a value slightly exceeding the cost of the works. The employer in such circumstances has an uphill task in attracting the sympathy of the court at Ord 14.

A notable feature of building contract litigation is the preponderance of cross-claims.

A set-off is a defence, and is treated as such for Ord 14 purposes. To be fully successful, however, it must at least match the amount of the claim. If the defendant establishes a set-off for a lesser amount of the claim, then the plaintiff has judgment for the balance (*Hanak v Green* [1958] 2 QB 9). It is not sufficient, however, for a defendant merely to allege the existence of a set-off; he must, subject to express contractual provisions, set up a plausible and properly quantified cross-claim if he is to extinguish or reduce his liability under Ord 14. The authority frequently quoted in support of this proposition is *Modern Engineering* v *Gilbert-Ash* [1973] 3 WLR 421, but this case must be read in the light of the express provision in the contract in question in the case entitling the defendants to raise any 'bona fide' set-off, and the court held this provision to allow the defendants a subjective test.

It was once thought following *Dawnays* v *FG Minter and Trollope & Colls* [1971] 1 WLR 1205 that there could be no set-off against an architect's certificate for payment but that such a certificate was to be treated like a bill of exchange. The *Minter* case was, however, overruled on this point by *Modern Engineering* v *Gilbert-Ash* [1973] 3 WLR 421, and there is now no rule precluding a defendant from resisting judgment at Ord 14 upon the ground of a sufficiently established set-off or counterclaim.

It is by no means clear what degree of proof is required from a defendant seeking to resist Ord 14 judgment by reference only to a set-off or a counterclaim. In practice, it seems to be much less than the degree of proof required by the plaintiff upon his claim and, although this proposition cannot be stated with any certainty, it may be that the result depends upon the court's view of the set-off or counterclaim as follows:

(1) If the court thinks that there is a genuine cross-claim, the cross-claim will operate to extinguish or reduce the defendant's liability at Ord 14 and leave to defend will be given accordingly.

(2) If the court is less convinced as to the validity of the cross-claim, it will give judgment for the plaintiff, stay execution upon that judgment and give directions as to the trial of the counterclaim.

(3) If it suspects, but cannot be sure, that the cross-claim is a

sham it will order the defendant to pay the amount of the plaintiff's claim into court, and give directions for the trial of the counterclaim.

A defendant cannot defend himself in Ord 14 proceedings by pointing to an arbitration clause in the contract. If the defendant has good grounds for a stay of proceedings under the Arbitration Act 1950, s 4, then the court will give judgment at Ord 14 for such part of the claim as falls within the scope of Ord 14, and only then grant the stay. In *Ellis Mechanical Services Ltd* v *Wates Construction Limited* (1976) 2 BLR 57 Lord Denning said:

> 'There is a point on the contract which I might mention upon this. There is a general arbitration clause. Any dispute or difference arising on the matter is to go to arbitration. It seems to me that if a case comes before the Court in which, although a sum is not exactly quantified and although it is not admitted, nevertheless the Court is able, on an application of this kind, to give summary judgment for such sum as appears to be indisputably due, and to refer the balance to arbitration. The defendants cannot insist on the whole going to arbitration by simply saying that there is a difference or a dispute about it. If the Court sees that there is a sum which is undisputably due, then the Court can give judgment for that sum and let the rest go to arbitration. . . .'

It is plain from the terms of Ord 14, r 1, that it is not necessary for the plaintiff to have quantified his claim if he is to obtain judgment under Ord 14. If he is able to establish the fact of the defendant's liability but not the amount of it then the court can give judgment for damages to be assessed.

Neither is it necessary for a plaintiff to seek Ord 14 judgment against all of several defendants. It is provided by Ord 14, r 8, that where a plaintiff obtains judgment against one defendant he may proceed with the action against any other defendant. This rule does not, however, overrule the cases summarised in the notes in the *White Book* at para 14/8/2A. A plaintiff must exercise especial care when obtaining judgment against a joint (cf joint and several) contractor, or an agent or principal.

It is, of course, no answer for a defendant merely to say that he has the right to be indemnified by some third party (*Thorne* v *Steel* [1878] WN 215 CA).

Conflicting decisions have been given as to whether or not the courts will consider difficult points of law at Ord 14. There are cases which suggest that leave to defend should be given where a difficult question of law is raised (*Electric & General Contract etc Corp* v *Thomson-Houston etc Co* (1893) 10 TLR 103); but if the court is satisfied that the defendant's point of law is really unarguable leave to defend will be refused (*Cow* v *Casey* [1949] 1 KB 481).

2 Procedure

The Ord 14 procedure cannot commence until the plaintiff has served a statement of claim (which may or may not have been indorsed on the writ) and the defendant has acknowledged service of the writ.

The procedure is commenced by the plaintiff issuing an Ord 14 summons. The plaintiff should follow the form of either Queen's Bench Master's practice form PF11 or PF12, according to whether the plaintiff seeks judgment for the whole of this claim or for part only. Those practice forms prescribe the following notice:

'Take notice that a party intending to oppose this application or to apply for a stay of execution should send to the opposite party or his solicitor, to reach him not less than three days before the date above-mentioned, a copy of any affidavit intended to be used.'

This is not a prescribed form, and there is no rule as such that the defendant must comply with this notice. See p 100.

Ordinarily, the plaintiff asks the court to mark the first available return date on the summons, which is usually a month or two ahead. Sometimes, however, where the plaintiff knows that the defendant will wish to defend the application and that a special appointment will, in any event, be necessary, this sometimes is issued in blank (that is to say, the court is asked to seal the summons but not to insert a return date). The return date is then arranged with the Master assigned by the Clerks of the counsel who are to appear.

It is usually in the plaintiff's interest to issue the summons as soon as the defendant has returned the acknowledgement of service. It is not necessary under the rules for the summons to be served immediately, provided that the summons is served not less than ten clear days before the return day set for the hearing (Ord 14, r 2) but the summons is usually served as soon as it is issued, not only as a matter of etiquette but also because the service of an Ord 14 summons suspends the obligation on the defendant to serve a defence (Ord 18, r 2(2)). Indeed, if the plaintiff serves an Ord 14 summons, not only need the defendant not serve his defence but he should not serve his defence until the summons is heard (*Hobson* v *Monks* [1884] WN 8).

The summons is not required to be served personally but may be served by pre-paid post at the address for service given by the defendant in the acknowledgement of service. The plaintiff's solicitor should, however, be careful to make a contemporaneous note as to the posting of the summons since an affidavit of service may later be required if the defendant does not acknowledge service or appear at the hearing of the Ord 14 summons.

Despite the note in the *White Book* at para 14/2/1, it is not necessary to delay the issue and the service of the summons until the affidavit in support is ready. The requirement under Ord 14, r 2(3), is that a summons, a copy of the affidavit in support and of any exhibits referred to therein must be served on the defendant not less than ten clear days before the return day. There is no requirement that all these documents must be served together.

It is rare for the court to abridge that ten clear days, and in some cases it may be appropriate to allow the defendant more than those ten clear days. The last moment for service can be calculated as follows:

Day of Return Day	Last Moment for Service is
Monday	Thursday at 4 pm
Tuesday	Friday at 4 pm
Wednesday	Saturday at 12 noon
Thursday	Saturday at 12 noon
Friday	Monday at 4 pm

Where the summons or affidavit is served by first class post there is a rebuttable presumption that is will have been delivered on the day after posting (Master's Practice Direction No 26A).

The affidavit should not be sworn before any solicitor or commissioner for oaths from the plaintiff's firm of solicitors (Ord 41, r 8).

The plaintiff's affidavit is not usually filed in court under Ord 41, r 9, before the hearing of the summons. The usual practice in the Queen's Bench Division is for the original affidavit and exhibits to be handed to the Master at the hearing of the summons, and the Master then automatically causes the affidavit to be filed after the hearing. The plaintiff's solicitor should, therefore, take at least two photocopies of the affidavit once it is sworn, one for service and the other for the use of the plaintiff's solicitor or counsel at and after the hearing of the summons.

Notwithstanding the notice on the Ord 14 summons requiring the defendant to serve his affidavit in reply not less than three days before the return date, there is no requirement in the Rules themselves to that effect. Indeed, there is no requirement that the defendant should serve an affidavit at all; under Ord 14, r 4(1), the defendant may show cause against the Ord 14 application 'by affidavit or otherwise to the satisfaction of the Court'. In practical terms, however, the situation is as follows:

   (i) The defendant must serve an affidavit before the hearing unless his answer to the Ord 14 application is a preliminary or technical one, not dependant upon any matter of fact or evidence;

(ii) If the defendant produces an affidavit at the Ord 14 hearing, but has not served the affidavit or an unsworn draft thereof at least three days before the hearing, then the Master will ordinarily give the plaintiff the choice between proceeding with the hearing as though the affidavit had been served in time or having an adjournment with the costs occasioned by the adjournment to be the plaintiff's in any event.

Unless a special appointment has been obtained for the hearing, then the summons is heard in Room 95 or 96, adjacent to the 'Bear Garden'. The plaintiff's solicitor hands in the summons, but not the affidavit, to the usher and then goes in with the defendant's solicitor to Room 95 or 96 to wait for the Master to call the case. If the summons is in the 10.30 list then counsel does not have the right of audience. At that time in the morning, Rooms 95 and 96 are crowded and sometimes noisy. It is not the occasion for sophisticated legal argument or lengthy explanation; the plaintiff has in practical terms about five minutes to persuade the Master to give judgment on the spot. If the Master is convinced within that time that he ought to give judgment under Ord 14, he will do so. If he is convinced that the case is not a proper one for Ord 14, he will dismiss the application. If he is unable to form any clear view without further consideration and argument, he will adjourn the hearing to a special appointment. It is not usually thought that he has power to adjourn the summons as such for hearing before an Official Referee, not at any rate unless both parties consent. The point, however, is not entirely clear and it may be arguable that the combined effect of Ord 14, r 6(1), and Ord 25, r 2(6), is that an Ord 14 summons may be adjourned for a hearing before the Official Referee in the same way that a summons for directions is so adjourned. What is clear, and indeed common, is that an Order granting leave to the defendant to defend is frequently coupled in building contract cases with a direction for transfer to the Official Referee for trial. The difference between adjourning the Ord 14 summons to the Official Referee and an Order for leave to defend with transfer for trial to the Official Referee can be a material one since it seems that a plaintiff will only rarely be allowed more than one application under Ord 14; see the cases referred to in the notes to the *White Book* at para 14/1/4.

There are cases where it is worthwhile for a plaintiff to do what he can to have his Ord 14 summons heard by an Official Referee rather than by a Master of the Queen's Bench Division. In particular, where a claim can only be readily understood by someone familiar with the scheme of the JCT contract and the detailed points of building contract law, then the experience of the Official Referee in these matters can be of great advantage to the plaintiff. All too often, a plaintiff finds that the Queen's Bench Masters become impatient with the tortuous provisions of the JCT contract, and the mere explanation of the standard form itself can be sufficient to persuade the Master that the case is too complicated for Ord 14.

There is no established practice for bringing an Ord 14 summons before an Official Referee at any early stage in the proceeding. The best course is probably for the plaintiff to desist from issuing an Ord 14 summons in the Queen's Bench corridor, doing his best to obtain an early transfer to the Official Referee, if possible by consent before service of the Defence, and then to issue an Ord 14 summons in the Official Referee's Court as soon as the action has been transferred.

3 The affidavit in support

There is a practice form (No PF10) for the plaintiff's affidavit in support of his Ord 14 summons. This practice form sets out the clauses which must be included in the affidavit, although of course further matters may appear.

The plaintiff's main objective in the drafting of the affidavit must be to show as strong a case as possible, as simply as possible, in order to try to minimise the opportunity for the defendant to confuse the issues in his affidavit in reply. It has been said that if the plaintiff needs to stray far from the practice form in order to show a prima facie case, then the case is already too complicated for Ord 14. That is probably an exaggeration, and plaintiffs sometimes succeed in obtaining Ord 14 judgment upon the strength of fairly lengthy Ord 14 affidavits, but the point remains that the plaintiff should keep the affidavit as short and as simple as possible. The affidavit should, as far as possible, be sharp and conclusive. To make lengthy explanations and apologies is to struggle in the quicksand.

Where the plaintiff is a contractor seeking payment due under a certificate, then the statement of claim should plead the date and amount of the certificate. The plaintiff should generally exhibit to his affidavit the certificate relied upon, but ordinarily should resist any temptation to explain why he feels that the certificate is correct. Where the contractor is suing for payment without a certificate, then he should usually exhibit his invoice or other demand for payment, but is not usually well advised to set out any further detailed justification for the amount of the sum claimed.

Where the plaintiff is an employer claiming in respect of defects, then the statement of claim should fully particularise the defects complained of. Where the plaintiff has clear documentary evidence as to the defects, such as a surveyor's report or an expression of dissatisfaction from the Building Inspector, then such evidence should generally be exhibited to the affidavit. Where the work has been already rectified by another contractor, then that other contractor's account should also be exhibited. The plaintiff should resist the temptation to exhibit evidence of peripheral matters, such as the contractor's insolence, his inefficiency, or his muddy boots.

To the extent that building contract litigation tends to raise a multiplicity of issues, it presents special problems for a plaintiff under Ord 14. As shown by *Ellis Mechanical Services Ltd* v *Wates Construction Ltd* (1976) 2 BLR 57 the courts do tend to recognise that problem and to make allowances. It is important for the plaintiff to recognise the underlying strength of his case, if there is one, and to stress that point. For example:

(1) Where a contractor has expended much money upon the performance of works, and been paid nothing for it, then the courts will be sympathetic at Ord 14, recognising that cash flow is the lifeblood of the industry.

(2) Where the employer has ordered extra works, or plainly hindered the contractor in the performance of those works, then the courts are quick to recognise that the contractor ought to be reimbursed.

(3) Where an architect appointed under a contract has certified that a contractor is entitled to a certain payment, or that the employer is entitled to certain liquidated damages for delay, then the court requires cogent evidence that such certificates ought not to be honoured.

(4) Where the claim comes from a sub-contractor then the courts are especially sceptical of defences raised by a main contractor who has yet to receive payment from the employer for some reason unconnected with the sub-contractor's work.

(5) Where an employer (or main contractor) has expended money rectifying the work of the contractor (or a sub-contractor) then the courts will readily infer that those works were, indeed, defective.

As a general rule, the function of the plaintiff's affidavit should be to focus attention upon the basic strength of the plaintiff's case and should steer clear of the side issues that abound in building contract cases.

4 The defendant's affidavit

The defendant usually has one or both of two objectives in mind when drafting his affidavit in reply;

(i) to show that his cross-claims are at least as substantial as the plaintiff's claim, and that it is quite likely that the plaintiff will eventually be ordered to pay the defendant money, rather than vice versa;

(ii) to show that the plaintiff's claim is speculative, and that it would be quite impossible to form any reliable view as to whether or not it will succeed until the final judgment.

It will not generally avail the defendant to show that there is an arbitration clause, or that the quantum of the plaintiff's claim may be in doubt, or that the defendant has some claim over against a third party, or that the defendant is short of money or expected a longer time before having to pay, or that the defendant would prefer more time to decide whether to pay or not. The defendant must bring before the court some matter which strikes at the very root of the plaintiff's claim.

There are two broad schools of thought as to how to achieve the objectives at (i) and (ii) above. Some defendants believe that the best means is to serve an extremely lengthy affidavit in reply, raising a large number of matters which either go to establish a cross-claim or which go to raise all sorts of issues as to whether the plaintiff's claim itself will succeed. In doing this, they hope to persuade the Master that the claim, while perhaps bona fide, is too complex or uncertain to be properly within the scope of Ord 14 and that it is only by trial in full that the court will be able to get to the bottom of the matter.

The other school of thought is that the defendant is best served by selecting one or two of his best points upon the basis that there may be other points upon which he will rely at trial but that these main points are, of themselves, sufficient to show that the case falls outside the scope of Ord 14.

There are advantages and disadvantages in each of these approaches, and it is impossible to say that either will always be preferable. The overwhelming advantage of the first approach is that it plays upon the tendency of Queen's Bench Division Masters to believe that they should not be plagued by complex building cases at Ord 14. A lengthy affidavit from the defendant may induce the plaintiff to serve a further lengthy affidavit in reply to it, and the defendant then points to the uncertainty and complexity of the case as self-evident. The main disadvantage with the first approach is that the defendant may be forced to scrape the bottom of the barrel to produce a sufficiently lengthy set of issues, and the Master may get the flavour that the defendant is demonstrating more ingenuity than merit. The good arguments are tarred with the same brush as the spurious arguments, and the Masters sometimes take it upon themselves to demonstrate that they are not fools to be fobbed off with a collection of lame excuses for non-payment.

The main danger of the second approach is that the plaintiff might be able to nullify effectively the one or two points chosen in argument or by an affidavit in reply, and the defendant may be left without further ammunition. There is, however, an advantage for the defendant to have referred in passing (without giving particulars) to other grounds of defence since this leaves the Master uncertain as to whether or not those other grounds might succeed. As a general rule, the court expects the defendant's affidavit to condescend upon particulars but the court does not always rigidly enforce this requirement where it sees that the defendant honestly, if erroneously, believes that some other main point would of itself suffice to defeat the application.

5 The plaintiff's affidavit in reply

There is no requirement for a plaintiff to serve any affidavit in reply to the defendant's affidavit, and if such an affidavit is served, it is not always necessary for the plaintiff to have it read at the hearing.

The plaintiff should be wary of serving an affidavit in reply. The basis of his application under Ord 14 is that the defendant has no arguable defence. If the plaintiff then argues upon the defendant's affidavit in reply he may defeat his own object.

Ordinarily, the plaintiff should only serve an affidavit in reply if, by doing so, he can concisely and convincingly demonstrate that some matter or matters raised by the defendant is or are spurious.

6 The order

The most common orders made under Ord 14 are to the following effect:

(1) that the plaintiff should have judgment for the whole of his claim;

(2) that the plaintiff should have judgment for a part of his claim, directions for trial being given as to the balance;

(3) that the defendant should have leave to defend the action but that the action be tried as a short cause;

(4) that the defendant's leave to defend the action should be conditional upon payment of the whole or part of the claim into court;

(5) that the plaintiff should have judgment upon his claim, but that execution be stayed pending trial of the defendant's counterclaim; or

(6) that the defendant should have leave to defend the whole action.

It can be seen that there are a variety of orders possible intermediate between outright success for one or other of the parties.

If a defendant is given leave to defend a building contract, in whole or in part, a direction is usually made for transfer to the Official Referee or, in the case of small cases, to a county court.

7 The appeal

It is comparatively easy to appeal from any judgment, order or decision of a Master of the Queen's Bench Division. Appeal lies to a judge (Ord 58, r 1(1)); and the judge hears the appeal de novo.

The notice of appeal must be issued within five days (or seven days if you count Saturdays, Sundays and Public Holidays) of the decision and served not less than two clear days before the day fixed before hearing the appeal (Ord 58, r 1(3)).

The issue of a notice of appeal does not, of itself, operate as a stay of execution of an Ord 14 judgment (Ord 58, r 1(4)) and the execution of a judgment under Ord 14 against a defendant frequently discourages that defendant from issuing or pursuing a notice of appeal.

8 Order 29, Part II

Until 1980 it was only possible for a plaintiff to obtain an order for interim payment on account of damages in respect of personal injuries or death, or in relation to claims for possession of land. Now, Ord 29 has been extensively widened in scope, and the court now has power in building contract cases to order interim payment where satisfied that the plaintiff would obtain a substantial judgment if the action proceeded to trial. The rules are set out at Ord 29, rr 9–18.

At the time of writing, it is too early to say what pattern will emerge under Ord 29, Pt II, in relation to building contract cases. It is specifically provided that an Ord 29, Pt II, application may be included in an Ord 14 summons (Ord 29, r 10(2)) and it may now be
* advisable to include an Ord 29, r 10, application with practically every Ord 14 application in a building contract case.

Unless there is an admission or a judgment, Ord 29, rr 11 and 12, provide that the court must be satisfied that if the action proceeded to trial the plaintiff would obtain judgment for substantial damages or for a substantial sum of money. How satisfied must the court be? Must it be satisfied beyond all doubt, beyond all reasonable doubt, or upon the balance of probabilities?

It may be that in practical terms there is no distinction between this test and the 'robust' approach suggested in *Ellis Mechanical Services Limited* v *Wates Construction Limited* (1976) 2 BLR 57, and that the practical effect of Ord 29, Pt II, will be to encourage the court to give judgment for an arbitrary part of the plaintiff's claim where it is difficult to identify a particular part of the claim which is beyond dispute. The court has express power under Ord 29, r 17, to order repayment of all or part of an interim payment under Ord 29, r 2, and this represents a marked difference between Ord 14 and Ord 29, Pt 11. It may well be that, in time, Ord 29, Pt II, will become as important or more important in building contract litigation than Ord 14.

It seems unlikely that a plaintiff will be able to avail himself of Ord 29, Pt II, in cases where the defendant successfully applies for a stay of proceedings under the Arbitration Act 1950, s 4, since the scheme of Ord 29, Pt II, is to allow the court to order an interim payment on account of a judgment eventually to be handed down *by the court*, and hence Ord 14 will probably remain the only available vehicle for a plaintiff who seeks a judgment from the courts before a matter is referred to arbitration.

Chapter 10
Section 4 Summonses

Building contracts frequently contain an arbitration clause which provides, in broad terms, that if there is a dispute between the parties then that dispute should be referred to arbitration. If there is such a clause, a party may nonetheless issue a writ in the High Court or take proceedings in the county court. If he does so, the defendant may, however, apply to the court for an order staying those court proceedings in order that an arbitration may take place. If the arbitration agreement is a domestic arbitration agreement, he does so under the Arbitration Act 1950, s 4(1), which provides as follows:

> 'If any party to an arbitration agreement, or any person claiming through or under him, commences any legal proceedings in any court against any other party to the agreement, or any person claiming through or under him, in respect of any matter agreed to be referred, any party to those legal proceedings may at any time after appearance, and before delivering any pleadings or taking any other step in the proceedings, apply to that court to stay the proceedings, and that court or a judge thereof, if satisfied that there is no sufficient reason why the matter should not be referred in accordance with that agreement, and that the applicant was, at the time when proceedings were commenced, and still remains, ready and willing to do all things necessary to the proper conduct of the arbitration, may make an order staying the proceedings.'

The court has a certain discretion under s 4, and there is substantial case law upon the circumstances in which the court will exercise that discretion. The plaintiff has a number of potential grounds upon which to resist a section 4 summons, and thereby keep the matter in the court. Those grounds are considered at p 110 et seq.

The burden of proof is twofold. In the first place, the defendant must show that he is within the scope of s 4. In practical terms, this means that he must show:

(i) the existence of a valid arbitration agreement covering the dispute;

(ii) that he has not delivered any legal pleadings or taken any other steps in the proceedings; and

(iii) that he was, at the time when the proceedings were commenced, and still remains ready and willing to do all things necessary to the proper conduct of the arbitration.

In the second place, if the defendant can satisfy the court as to these matters, the burden of proof shifts to the plaintiff to show that there is a material reason why the matter should not be referred to arbitration.

Where there is an international element in the arbitration agreement, such that it is not a domestic arbitration agreement within the meaning of the Arbitration Act 1975, s 1(4), then the position is different. Whereas under the Arbitration Act 1950, s 4, the court *may* stay the court proceedings, under the Arbitration Act 1975, s 1, the court *shall* stay the court proceedings. The relevant parts of the Arbitration Act 1975, s 1, are as follows:

> '1—(1) If any party to an arbitration agreement to which this section applies, or any person claiming through or under him, commences any legal proceedings in any court against any other party to the agreement, or any person claiming through or under him, in respect of any matter agreed to be referred, any party to the proceedings may at any time after appearance, and before delivering any pleadings or taking any other steps in the proceedings, apply to the court to stay the proceedings; and the court, unless satisfied that the arbitration agreement is null and void, inoperative or incapable of being performed or that there is not in fact any dispute between the parties with regard to the matter agreed to be referred, shall make an order staying the proceedings.
>
> (2) This section applies to any arbitration agreement which is not a domestic arbitration agreement; and neither s 4(1) of the Arbitration Act 1950 nor s 4 of the Arbitration Act (Northern Ireland) 1937 shall apply to an arbitration agreement to which this section applies.
>
> (3) . . .
>
> (4) In this section 'domestic arbitration agreement' means an arbitration agreement which does not provide, expressly or by implication, for arbitration in a State other than the United Kingdom and to which neither:
>
> (*a*) an individual who is a national of, or habitually resident in, any State other than the United Kingdom; nor
>
> (*b*) a body corporate which is incorporated in, or whose central management and control is exercised in, any State other than the United Kingdom;
>
> is a party at the time the proceedings are commenced.'

For the effect of the Arbitration Act 1975, s 1, see p 155 and the case of *Associated Bulk Carriers* v *Koch Shipping* (1977) 7 BLR 18.

In addition to its powers under the Arbitration Act 1950, s 4, and the Arbitration Act 1975, s 1, the High Court has an inherent jurisdiction to stay proceedings under the Supreme Court of Judicature (Consolidation) Act 1925, s 41 (*Roussel-Uclaf* v *G D Searle & Co Ltd* [1978] 1 Lloyds Rep 225). Section 41 provides as follows:

'**41**—No cause or proceedings at any time pending in the High Court or the Court of Appeal shall be restrained by prohibition or injunction, but every matter of equity on which an injunction against the prosecution of any such cause or proceeding might formerly have been obtained, whether unconditionally or on any terms or conditions, may be relied on by way of defence thereof:

Provided that—

(*a*) nothing in this Act shall disable either of the said Courts if it thinks fit so to do, from directing a stay of proceedings in any cause or matter pending before it; and

(*b*) any person, whether a party or not to any such cause or matter, who would formerly have been entitled to apply to any Court to restrain the prosecution thereof, or who may be entitled to enforce, by attachment or otherwise, any judgment, decree, rule or order, in contravention of which all or any part of the proceedings in the cause or matter have been taken, may apply to the High Court or the Court of Appeal, as the case may be, by motion in a summary way, for a stay of proceedings in the cause or matter, either generally, or so far as may be necessary for the purposes of justice, and the Court shall thereupon make such order as may be just.'

A commentary upon the Supreme Court of Judicature (Consolidation) Act 1925, s 41, appars at para 3345 et seq of Part 2 of the *White Book*. It is not usual to rely upon this section when seeking a stay upon the ground of a domestic arbitration agreement since the court has a wide discretion under the Arbitration Act 1950, s 4. A commentary to s 4 appears at para 3714 et seq of Part 2 of the *White Book*.

1 Practice

If a defendant is sued in relation to a contract containing an arbitration clause, he should decide as quickly as possible whether he is content to have the matter heard in the court or whether he wishes to have the matter referred to arbitration. If the latter is chosen, he should issue his Section 4 summons as soon as possible after acknowledging service of the writ. The reference in s 4 to 'appearance' should now be regarded as a reference to 'acknowledgement of service' (Ord 12, r 10).

The application under s 4 is made by summons. There is no prescribed form for this summons; a typical wording is:

. . . for an order that these proceedings be stayed pursuant to s 4 of the Arbitration Act 1950, and that the plaintiffs do pay the defendants the costs of these proceedings, including the costs of this application.

Although not prescribed, an affidavit is also required in practice from the defendant, and the affidavit should include the matters in respect of which the burden of proof rests upon the defendant; see p 108.

Save that there is a general rule that summonses should be served two clear days before the return day (Ord 32, r 3), there is no express guidance in the court rules as to when the summons and the affidavit should be served. In practice, however, it is generally thought that a minimum of several days is appropriate and it is reasonable to allow the plaintiff time to prepare and serve an affidavit in reply.

In the first instance, the application is heard by a Master. As is the case with Ord 14 summonses, section 4 summonses are often returnable in the first place on an ordinary appointment, but a special appointment is necessary if there is to be any lengthy argument.

It is an anomaly of the rules of the Supreme Court that there is no provision for an automatic extension of time for service of a defence where a defendant issues a section 4 summons. It is, however, universally accepted that the issue of a section 4 summons does have this effect.

It frequently happens that a defendant issues a section 4 summons after the plaintiff has issued an Ord 14 summons, or that a plaintiff issues an Ord 14 summons after the defendant has issued a section 4 summons. In these cases, it is appropriate for both summonses to be heard at the same time, and an ex parte application should be made to the Master assigned for leave to make the second summons returnable at the same time as the first. Further, it is common for a plaintiff to make a single affidavit in support of his Ord 14 application and in opposition to the defendant's section 4 summons, and for the defendant to make a single affidavit in opposition to the Ord 14 summons and in support of his section 4 summons.

2 No step in the proceedings

The defendant should issue his section 4 summons 'before delivering any pleadings or taking any other steps in the proceedings'. If he has taken a step in the proceedings, that is usually fatal to him.

The question of what is and what is not a 'step' has been the subject of much litigation; the leading cases are reviewed at para 3715 of Part 2 in the *White Book*. The taking out of a time summons by the defendant does constitute a step in the action *(Fords Hotel v Bartlett* [1896] AC 1) but it is clear that it is not a step in the action for a defendant merely to write to the plaintiff asking for an extension of time and obtaining it (*Brighton Marine Etc Co v Woodhouse* [1893] 2 Ch 486). It is not unknown for a plaintiff's solicitor to refuse an extension of time with the specific hope that the defendant will take out a time summons and thereby lose the chance of having the action stayed under s 4. Opposition to an Ord 14 summons may constitute a step in the action, but a defendant does not take a step in the action by serving an affidavit in reply to an Ord 14 summons after or at the same time as issuing a section 4 summons (*Pitchers Limited v Plaza (Queensbury) Limited* [1940] 1 All ER 151).

The article at para 3715 of Part 2 of the *White Book* suggests:

'The distinction seems to be that negotiation or correspondence between parties or their solicitors does not constitute a step in the action, but an application by summons or motion, or the service of a pleading does.'

It appears, however, that the courts are now drawing the dividing line in a different way. In *Eagle Star Insurance Co Ltd v Yuval Insurance Co Ltd* [1978] 1 Lloyds Rep 357 the defendants' application to strike out the plaintiffs' endorsement on the writ was found not to constitute a step in the action. Lord Denning said:

'What then is a "step in the proceedings"? It has been discussed in several cases. On principle it is a step by which the defendant evinces an election to abide by the Court proceedings and waives his right to ask for an arbitration. Like any election, it must be an equivocal act done with knowledge of the material circumstances . . .
'A "step in the proceedings" must be one which impliedly affirms the correctness of the proceedings and the willingness of the defendant to go along with a determination by the courts of law instead of arbitration.'

Again, in *Roussel-Uclaf v G D Searle & Co Ltd* [1978] 1 Lloyds Rep 225 it was found that the defendants had not taken a step in the action by defending an application for an interlocutory injunction.

3 Ready and willing

The defendant must show that he was, at the time when the proceedings were commenced, and still remains, ready and willing to do all things necessary to the proper conduct of the arbitration. This should appear from his affidavit in support (*Piercy v Young* [1879] 14 ChD 209).

There is a point upon limitation which has been argued more than once. It is as follows. It sometimes happens that a plaintiff issues a writ in the High Court at the last moment. The writ is sometimes not served for some time, and the limitation period has expired by the time the defendant issues a section 4 summons. The plaintiff then realises that he has overlooked the Limitation Act 1980, s 34, which provides that for the purposes of arbitration proceedings, the test is whether or not the claimant has served a notice upon the respondent requiring him to concur in the appointment of an arbitrator. The claim would therefore be statute barred in any arbitration proceedings. The plaintiff then asks the defendant whether he would waive any limitation point in arbitration proceedings, and the defendant declines to make any such waiver. The plaintiff then argues at the hearing of the section 4 summons that the defendant, by declining to make that waiver, is not ready and willing to do all things necessary to the proper conduct of the arbitration. This argument generally fails upon the authority of *W Bruce Limited* v *J Strong* [1951] 2 KB 447. The authority of the *Bruce* case is, however, weakened partly by the fact that the Court of Appeal declined to follow it upon another point in *Taunton-Collins* v *Crombie* [1964] 1 WLR 633, and partly because of the terms of the particular arbitration clause in question. Indeed, it seems that *Bruce* v *Strong* was not followed by Bean J in *County and District Properties* v *Jenner*, although the point is not entirely clear from the report of the later judgment of Swanwick J, reported at [1976] 2 Lloyds Rep 728.

A defendant may well be unable to show his willingness to do all things necessary to the proper conduct of the arbitration if he has declined to execute the RIBA's standard form of application for the appointment of an arbitrator; see p 150. A defendant should not be so keen to show his readiness and willingness to proceed with the arbitration as to encourage an arbitrator to proceed with an arbitration pending the hearing of a section 4 summons (*Doleman & Sons* v *Ossett Corporation* [1912] 3 KB 257).

4 No dispute

The defendant cannot insist on a matter going to arbitration where there is no dispute between the parties as to that matter (*Nova (Jersey) Knit Ltd* v *Kammgarn Spenneri GmbH* [1977] 1 WLR 713). There is authority for the proposition that this principle is widely applied in building contract cases. In *Ellis Mechanical Services Ltd* v *Wates Construction Limited* (1976) 2 BLR 57 Lord Denning said:

'There is a point on the contract which I might mention upon this. There is a general arbitration clause. Any dispute or difference arising on the matter is to go to arbitration. It seems to me that if a case comes before the court in which, although a sum is not exactly quantified and although it is not admitted, nevertheless the court is able, on an application of this kind, to give summary judgment for such sum as appears to be indisputably due, and to refer the balance to arbitration. The defendant cannot insist on the whole going to arbitration by simply saying that there is a difference or dispute about it. If the court sees that there is a sum which is indisputably due, then the court can give judgment for that sum and let the rest go to arbitration.'

The test as to whether there is a dispute for the purposes of s 4 is the same as the test under Ord 14, and it is relevant to consider the 'robust approach' suggested by Lawton LJ in *Ellis Mechanical Services Ltd* v *Wates Construction Limited*:

'The courts are aware what happens in these building disputes; cases go either to arbitration or before an Official Referee; they drag on and on and on; the cash flow is held up. In the majority of cases, because one party or the other cannot wait any longer for the money, there is some kind of compromise, very often not based on the justice of the case but on the financial situation of one of the parties. That sort of result is to be avoided if possible. In my judgment it can be avoided if the court makes a robust approach, as the Master did in this case, to the jurisdiction under Ord 14.'

It is clear from the judgments that if appropriate the courts will give Ord 14 judgment for part of the claim, and refer the balance to arbitration. In *Associated Bulk Carriers* v *Koch Shipping* (1977) 7 BLR 18 (a case under the Arbitration Act 1975) the Court of Appeal found itself unable to split the claim in this way. Differing views have been expressed as to this case; the editors of *Building Law Reports* suggest that it illustrates the limits of the principles enunciated in the *Ellis* case, whereas *Keating* suggests that the position is different under the Arbitration Act 1975 (see p 155). The editors of the *White Book* suggest that the decision in *Associated Bulk Carriers* has now been negatived by the new provisions as to interim payment in Ord 29, Pt II, but, with respect, it seems unlikely that Ord 29, Pt II, can apply to a case destined for arbitration.

5 The arbitration agreement

A defendant will succeed in obtaining a stay of the court proceedings under s 4 only if the court is satisfied that there is a valid arbitration agreement, and further that all (or all but a small part) of the relief claimed is within the scope of the arbitration agreement (*Ives & Barker* v *Willans* [1894] 2 Ch 478).

If there is a genuine dispute as to whether the contract (or the part of the contract which contains the arbitration clause) has ever regulated the legal position between the parties, the courts will not generally stay the court proceedings. In *Heyman* v *Darwins Limited* [1942] AC 356, the House of Lords said:

> 'If the dispute is whether the contract which contains the clause has ever been entered into at all, that issue cannot go to arbitration under the clause, for the party who denies that he has ever entered into the contract is thereby denying that he has ever joined in the submission. Similarly, if one party to the alleged contract is contending that it is void ab initio (because for example, the making of such a contract is illegal), the arbitration clause cannot operate for on this view the clause itself is also void.'

The position is, however, different where one party (or both) allege that the contract has been repudiated, for an arbitrator does have jurisdiction to decide upon this point (*Heyman* v *Darwins Limited*).

6 Multiplicity of proceedings

Where the facts give rise not only to a dispute between the plaintiff and the defendant, but also to disputes involving third parties then that is a factor that tilts the balance of convenience against arbitration, since it is rarely possible to have all the disputes heard effectively in the same arbitration. The court recognises the increased cost and danger of split findings if these claims cannot be heard together, and the involvement of more than two parties in a dispute generally dissuades the court from ordering a stay of the court proceedings (*Taunton-Collins* v *Crombie* [1964] 1 WLR 633).

7 Question of law

Where the dispute involves or substantially involves a question of law that may be a factor to influence the court to refuse to stay the court proceedings. There are conflicting decisions upon this point. It has been said that a point upon the construction of a clause in a civil engineering contract should be tried by an arbitrator because of the relevance of custom and technical terms (*Metropolitan Tunnel etc Ltd* v *London Electric Railway* [1926] Ch 371). Conversely, it was said in *Martin* v *Selsdon (No 2)* (1950) 67 RPC 64 that it may be bad practice to permit matters of construction of building contracts to go to arbitration; and in *Bristol Corporation* v *John Aird Limited* [1913] AC 241 the House of Lords said:

> 'Everybody knows that with regard to the construction of an agreement it is absolutely useless to stay the action because it will only come back to the court on a case stated.'

The practical effect of these conflicting decisions appears to be that the court has a free hand in each case to decide whether a point of law ought to be tried in the courts or by arbitration.

8 Fraud

Where a dispute arises as to whether a party has been guilty of fraud, then the High Court has express power under s 24(2) and (3) to refuse to stay any court proceedings.

9 Impartiality of arbitrator

Where the arbitration agreement names or designates the arbitrator the High Court has an express power under the Arbitration Act 1950, s 24(1) and (3), to refuse to stay the High Court proceedings upon the ground that the arbitrator is not or may not be impartial.

10 Legal aid

Where a plaintiff does not himself have the necessary funds to pay the legal costs of an action, and requires legal aid, it can work great hardship on him if his claim is referred to arbitration since legal aid is not available in arbitrations. It was held in *Smith* v *Pearl Assurance Co* [1939] 1 All ER 95 that the poverty of a litigant is not a ground for keeping the dispute in the court. In *Fakes* v *Taylor Woodrow Limited* [1973] QB 436, however, the plaintiff showed that his poverty was caused by the defendant itself, and he was accordingly allowed to keep his dispute in the court where legal aid was available to him.

11 Delay

The courts are often alive to the fact that defendants sometimes take out section 4 summonses with a view to taking advantage of the delay inherent in arbitration proceedings. As to the court's view of the merits of that tactic, see *Associated Bulk Carriers Ltd* v *Koch Shipping Inc* (1977) 7 BLR 18.

Where the court finds that the object of the defendant in issuing the section 4 summons is indeed to delay the plaintiff, a stay of the court proceedings may be refused (*Lury* v *Pearson* (1856) 1 CB (NS) 639).

Article 5.2 of the JCT contract provides that a reference to arbitration shall not be 'opened' prior to completion without the consent of both parties. Differing views have been expressed as to the meaning of this obscure wording, and different views have been expressed as to whether a party loses his right to arbitration if he withholds his consent (see *Gilbert Ash Limited* v *Modern Engineer-*

ing (Bristol) Limited [1974] AC 689 and *Mitchell Construction Limited* v *East Anglian Regional Hospital Board* (1966, unreported)). *

Chapter 11
Official Referees' Business

* Strictly speaking, the office of 'Official Referee' was abolished by the Courts Act 1971. The term 'Official Referee' is however universally used to describe such circuit judges as the Lord Chancellor has from time to time determined shall discharge the functions conferred on Official Referees in accordance with the rules of Ord 36.

*   There are three Official Referees in London:
- (i) His Honour Judge Sir William Stabb QC, senior judge assigned to Official Referee's business (Court 28) (*Clerk:* Mr FCG Wheeler, room 742; *Rota clerk:* Ms BL Joy, room 742)
- (ii) His Honour Judge Lewis Hawser QC (Court 30) (*Clerk:* Mrs PM Bevan, room 724)
- (iii) His Honour Judge John Newey QC (Court 29) (*Clerk:* Mr CT Charalambides, room 741)

The courts of the Official Referees and the offices of their clerks, are all to be found in a long corridor on the third floor of the West Block of the Royal Courts of Justice in the Strand. The following directions may be helpful:
- (i) Enter the Courts by the main entrance in the Strand.
- (ii) Turn left immediately after the security desks into a short corridor leading off the main hall.
- (iii) At the end of that corridor turn left.
- (iv) Then turn right up some steps past room 535.
- (v) Turn right again at room 536.
- (vi) Take the lift to the third floor.
- (vii) At third floor pass through the mauve doors and turn left. You are now at the south end of the Official Referees' corridor, not far from the Courts of Judge Stabb and Judge Newey. The Court of Judge Hawser is to be found at the north end of the corridor, after the kink.

The Official Referees' Court shares the same telephone number as the rest of the building, 01-405 7641, and it is quite possible to speak by telephone to the clerk to the Official Referee assigned to the case in question.

In practice, the Official Referee's Court is usually regarded as a sub-division of the Queen's Bench Division, although a few cases are taken from the Chancery Division. The Official Referee assigned to the case normally takes all hearings, and therefore acts as both Master and Judge. The clerk to the assigned Official Referee performs substantially all the administrative functions with regard to the case, such as maintaining the court file, issuing summonses, sealing orders and acting as the court's associate during hearings.

Proceedings in the Official Referee's Court are marked by an informality as though they were a hybrid between arbitration proceedings and other proceedings in the Queen's Bench Division. The clerks are able, because of their extensive functions, to be particularly helpful.

The Official Referees are addressed as 'Your Honour' whether sitting in chambers or in open court. Solicitors and their clerks do have, and often exercise, rights of audience at hearings in chambers, and indeed it is quite common at interlocutory hearings for solicitors and counsel to appear facing each other. Neither the Official Referees nor the advocates appear robed at interlocutory hearings, but they do at trial.

Once an action has been transferred to the Official Referee, no further applications are normally to be made in the Queen's Bench corridor. At least one Official Referee usually sits from time to time during the long vacation, although the Masters of the Queen's Bench Division have jurisdiction during long vacations (Ord 64, r 6(2)). The note at the second paragraph of 36/6/1 in the *White Book* is regarded as wrong in suggesting that Masters of the Queen's Bench Division have any more extensive jurisdiction than this.

In the past, Official Referees have sometimes expressed their willingness to hear Ord 14 applications even at a comparatively advanced stage in the proceedings. Now Ord 29, Pt II, has been extensively enlarged in its scope, it may be that the Official Referees will be willing, in an appropriate case, to make an order for interim payment. A plaintiff may now be well advised to keep Ord 29, Pt II, continually in mind, especially if it seems that the Official Referee has come to believe that the plaintiff will recover in whole or in part at trial.

1 Procedure on transfer to the Official Referee   *

Where a Master in the Queen's Bench Division makes an order for trial of an action before an Official Referee, that is tantamount to an order that the action be transferred to the Official Referees' Court. The reference is treated as equivalent to setting the matter down for trial for the purposes of the Supreme Court Fees Order 1980 (SI 1980 No 827).

The order for transfer is drawn up in the Queen's Bench corridor in the usual way. It is then usually regarded as the function of the plaintiff's solicitors to give effect to that order by attending the clerk to the senior Official Referee. The Official Referees' Court has issued the following notes as to the procedure:

*

HIGH COURT OF JUSTICE
OFFICIAL REFEREE'S BUSINESS
PROCEDURE (ORDER 36 R.S.C.)

1. When an Order referring a matter to an Official Referee has been made and drawn up, bring to Room 742 (Rota Clerk) the following:
   (a) Original Writ and Copy
   (b) Original Order referring the matter and Copy
   (c) Praecipe E.26 (from Room 117) stamped £20 (unless action has been previously set down for trial elsewhere and fee was paid then)
2. The matter will be allocated to a particular Official Referee by the Rota Clerk.
3. At the same time or within 14 days thereafter:
   (d) If Liberty to Restore allowed on (b) 2 copies of the original summons should be provided, a fresh date for Directions before the Official Referee will then be endorsed.
       If the original summons did not allow for Liberty to Restore, then 2 copies of Judge's Summons (Form S.1) are required (Suitable wording being; '. . . for further [or General] directions . . .')
   (e) Copy Pleadings (one set starting with further copy of Writ).
4. All orders to be drawn up should be brought *in duplicate* with the summons to the Clerk to the Official Referee to whom the matter has been allocated at No. 2 above.
5. Short (5 min) summonses issued by Rota Clerk; others after consultation with appropriate Judge's clerk (summonses *in duplicate*).

Although it is regarded as the duty of the plaintiff's solicitor to effect the transfer (Notes to the *White Book*, para 36/5/1) the plaintiff is sometimes unwilling to do so. In such circumstances it is open to the defendant to effect the transfer if he so wishes, although he should normally obtain the original writ from the plaintiff's solicitor and pay the setting down fee.

Form E26 is not a practice form. It is supplied free from Room 117, and is set out as follows:

E.26   *Praecipe—Entry of Action for Trial*

IN THE HIGH COURT OF JUSTICE 19   ,   ,   No.

Division

BETWEEN

Plaintiff,

and

Defendant

Enter this

Dated the   day of   19

(Signed)
(Address)

---

2 The application for directions

Within fourteen days after the allocation of the business to a particular Official Referee an application for directions should be made to the Official Referee in question (Ord 36, r 6(2)). The obligation to make that application falls upon whichever party produced the order for transfer to the Rota Clerk, and if that party does not make the application in time any other interested party in the action may do so, or apply to the Official Referee to strike out the others' pleadings (Ord 36, r 6(3)). Such an application to strike out the others' pleadings may be (and in practice usually is) treated as the missing application for directions itself (Ord 36, r 6(4)).

The first application for directions is treated in much the same way as a preliminary meeting before an arbitrator or a summons for directions in the Queen's Bench corridor. In a practice direction issued in 1968 by Sir Walker Carter, then the senior Official Referee, the following guidance appeared:

1 At the time of the issue of the first summons before the Official Referee, a copy of all pleadings, including particulars, already served should be lodged with his Clerk so that they can be considered by the Official Referee before the hearing of the summons. Such copy of the pleadings may be collected from the Clerk to the Official Referee for the purpose of preparing a bound copy of the pleadings for use at the trial.

2 At the hearing of the first summons before the Official Referee, the solicitors of the parties or their London agents should be in the position to state the nature of the claim and of the defence. (Failure in this respect may result in unnecessary adjournments with attendant costs.)

3   At the hearing of the first summons before him, the Official Referee will give the necessary directions and make the necessary orders regarding the steps in the action to be taken by the parties. It is of the utmost importance that these steps should be taken within the time-limits set by the directions or order, so that the practice of giving a fixed date for the trial may be continued.

4   Once the action has been given a fixed date for trial, no alteration will be granted except with the leave of the Official Referee, which will be granted only in exceptional circumstances. If a fixed date for trial is vacated, the fresh date for trial may not be a fixed date.

5   Where a party intends to adduce expert evidence, he should produce to the other party his expert statement of proposed evidence, together with any reports, plans, models, calculations, etc, relevant to it, for agreement if possible. Failing such agreement, the other party should deliver to the first party a written statement setting out particulars of the matters not agreed. Where both parties intend to adduce expert evidence, each should follow this procedure. Failure by any party to follow this procedure may result in a special order as to costs.

Paragraph 5 of this practice direction has been substantially overtaken by the Civil Evidence Act 1972, and the rules that now appear in Ord 38, Pt IV. The rest of the practice direction, which substantially relates to the first summons for directions, is however still treated as having force. An unprepared or unintelligent approach to the application for directions will not impress the Official Referee, and it is not usually advisable for a solicitor to delegate appearance at the application to an inexperienced clerk. Indeed, it is not uncommon for counsel to appear on this application.

The following issues are likely to arise on the application for directions, and it is worth giving thought to them before the summons:

1   The 'main' pleadings. Where the reference to the Official Referee is made on the hearing of an application for judgment under Ord 14, then the only pleading served may be the Statement of Claim. If so, then the Official Referee will normally make orders for the time for service of subsequent pleadings.

2   Schedules. In addition to the main pleadings, the Official Referee frequently orders preparation of a Scott Schedule (see p 124). The Official Referee frequently makes orders as to the form and timing of the schedule on this first summons before him.

Sometimes, the precise form of the Schedule is of particular importance, and it may be in the interests of one party to make sure that the headings are prescribed by the court rather than left to the other party. For example, an employer defending a disruption claim may be able to get an order requiring the contractor to particularise in schedule form precisely which loss and expense results from precisely which matter complained of. This may be an impossible task for the contractor where all the contractor can do is point to the totality of his loss. Likewise, where an employer makes complaint of a very large number of defects, the contractor may seek to require the employer to particularise in schedule form the probable cause of every defect alleged. Again, this can sometimes be an unanswerable question. For these reasons, it is highly desirable that each party's representative at the summons should know what particulars his client can give, and with what difficulty, and should also have a view as to what his opponent's clients will be able to particularise, and with what difficulty.

3 It is usually at this summons that the Official Referee makes orders for discovery and inspection of documents. It is not usually fatal to a party if he fails to meet the first deadline for discovery and inspection. Indeed it is fairly rare for him to do so. It is however worth bearing in mind that the court is not impressed where the representatives of the parties cannot or do not make realistic estimates for the time necessary for discovery at the outset.

4 Experts. It is often premature at the time of the first summons to reach a final view as to the desirability of expert evidence. Nevertheless, orders are frequently made at this stage and the representatives of the parties should arm themselves with the answers to the following questions:

(a) Might my clients wish to call expert evidence?

(b) If so, how many experts will be necessary?

(c) When will those experts' reports be ready, bearing in mind the need to consider them after receipt from the expert and before delivery to the other side? The parties should also bear in mind that leave to call expert evidence at trial is usually made conditional on their reports being furnished to the other parties at a fixed date before the trial.

5 Trial Date. The practice of the Official Referee's Court is to set a trial date at the hearing of the first summons before it. Where the parties are represented by solicitors, it is well worthwhile therefore for those solicitors to establish from counsel's Clerk the state of that counsel's diary over the next

year. Many specialist counsel have trial dates marked in their
diaries for a year or even two years hence and indeed for
some periods may be double-booked or even treble-booked.
Many of those dates will become inoperative by reason of
settlements of other cases and it is rarely possible to form an
accurate picture of when any individual counsel will be
available. Usually, however, some dates are plainly more
difficult than others, and where a party's counsel has difficulty with a trial date put forward by the court then he should
say so to the court immediately. The parties' representative
should, of course, be in a position to estimate as accurately as
possible the likely length of trial.

6   Other Matters. This summons is the appropriate time for the
parties to raise any other matter with the court which they
would have raised at the summons for directions in an
ordinary case in the Queen's Bench Division.

Under the rules of the Supreme Court there are certain things
which must be done within a certain period after setting down for
trial. In particular, a notice to admit facts under Ord 27, r 2, should
be served not later than twenty-one days after the action is set down
for trial. Likewise, a notice of desire to give hearsay evidence under
Ord 38, r 1, ought to be given within twenty-one days after setting
down. The rules are not explicit about when an Official Referee's
matter is deemed to be 'set down' for these purposes and in any
event, the twenty-one days are not usually regarded as a rigid
time-limit.

The notice to admit facts, in particular, can be a powerful weapon
and the time to consider using it is not later than the first summons
before the Official Referee.

As soon as possible after the hearing it is the responsibility of the
party who made the application (usually the plaintiff) to draw up the
order. This is done by drawing up the order made and taking two
copies of this plus the summons itself to the Clerk to the Official
Referee, who usually will have been in court at the time the order
was made. The Clerk then seals the order and retains one copy. It is
for the party drawing up the order to serve copies of it on the other
parties after it has been sealed.

3 Scott Schedules

When a matter is transferred to the Official Referee the pleadings
will usually be closed within the meaning of Ord 18, r 20. It is,
however, very common for the Official Referee to order further
pleadings in the form of an Official Referee's Schedule, or 'Scott

Schedule' as it is popularly known. Scott Schedules should be seen as ancillary to the main pleadings and are in the nature of further and better particulars set out in tabular form.

Scott Schedules can take various forms. They are usually pleadings in tabular form (often typed on large sheets of paper) where the contentions of the plaintiff and the defendant and the comments of the Official Referee can all be marked side by side in columns.

Scott Schedules are used both in respect of claims by contractors for payment, and in respect of claims by employers for defects. In the former case, a typical layout for the columns, from left to right, is as follows:

1 Paragraph number;
2 Description of item of work;
3 Plaintiff's comments;
4 Amount of plaintiff's claim;
5 Defendant's comments;
6 Price (if any) conceded by the defendant;
7 Official referee's comments;
8 Official referee's price; and
9 VAT.

In the case of a claim by an employer for defects, a typical layout is as follows:

1 Paragraph number;
2 Defect alleged by plaintiff;
3 Sum claimed by plaintiff;
4 Defendant's comments;
5 Defendant's estimate of the cost of remedial work;
6 Official referee's comments;
7 Damages awarded.

The form of these Schedules can vary considerably. The Official Referee usually specifies in his order which party is responsible for preparing the first part of the Schedule, and which party must reply to that. He does not usually prescribe the form of the Schedule but leaves it to the good sense of the parties. Sometimes, however, it is appropriate to ask the Official Referee to specify in his order the precise form of the Schedule. Certainly, the form of the Schedule can make a party's task in preparing his part of the Scott Schedule comparatively easy or comparatively difficult. For example, it would often be extremely difficult for a contractor to set out a claim for an extension of time under the JCT contract if he were required to complete the following columns:

1 Paragraph number;
2 Cause of delay alleged;

3 Date of notice under clause 25.2.1.1;
4 Date of delivery of notice to nominated subcontractors under clause 25.2.1.2;
5 Date of particulars under clause 25.2.2.1;
6 Date of estimate under clause 25.2.2.2;
7 Dates of further notices under clause 25.2.3;
8 Particulars of contractors best endeavours under clause 25.3.4.1; and
9 Subclause of clause 25.4 relied on by the contractor.

A contractor would be strongly advised not to agree to prepare his part of the Scott Schedule in this form, for in doing so he would take upon himself a burden of proof so heavy that the mere research needed for the pleading would, in a complex case, be well nigh impossible.

Precedents for Scott Schedules can be found in *Keating*, and in the standard court precedent books.

4 Appeals from the Official Referee

An appeal lies to the Court of Appeal from a decision of an official referee:

(i) on a point of law;
(ii) as to cost only; and
(iii) on a question of fact relevant to a charge of fraud or professional duty (Ord 58, r 5).

Generally speaking, an appeal does not lie from the Official Referee upon any other judgment, order or decision. Appeal does, however, lie from the exercise of discretion by an Official Referee, since this is a point of law (*Instrumatic Limited* v *Supabrase Limited* [1969] 1 WLR 519). Likewise, a decision as to the facts may be appealed if the appellant can establish 'either that there was no evidence to support it, or that is was in reality simply an inference from certain primary facts, and that, as such, it was wholly un-warrantable. In either of these events a point of law arises. . . .' (*Peak* v *McKinney* (1970) 1 BLR 114).

It was said in *Technistudy Limited* v *Kelland* [1976] 1 WLR 1042 that leave to appeal is not necessary for an appeal on a point of law against the decision of an Official Referee, but this case (and indeed Ord 58, r 5, itself) must be read subject to the Supreme Court of Judicature (Consolidation) Act 1925, s 31, which (in broad terms) provides that leave is needed to appeal from:

(i) a consent order (s 31(1)(*h*));
(ii) an order as to costs only (s 31(1)(*h*)); and
(ii) most interlocutory judgments and orders (s 31(1)(*i*)).

Chapter 12
Pleadings

Pleadings do not, of course, have the importance they once had. Nevertheless, a properly pleaded statement of claim is a great advantage if it is intended to seek judgment at Ord 14, and if a party does not have his pleadings in order until the last moment before trial he may be forced into a lengthy adjournment or, where the limitation period has already expired, lose his claim altogether.

Pleadings of complexity are usually settled by counsel. That said, it is of great importance for those instructing counsel to understand thoroughly any pleadings settled by counsel. Counsel do sometimes overlook points, and solicitors are at a grave disadvantage at subsequent interlocutory stages if they do not fully understand the case that has been put forward on their client's behalf in the pleadings. In simple cases, it is common for the pleadings to be settled by solicitors. That has the advantage of being quicker and cheaper, but care should be taken to ensure that the pleading comprehends the true nature of the case being put forward.

There follow four precedents which set out the typical form of statements of claim in certain circumstances.

Precedent 1
Statement of Claim for payment under quantum meruit

The Plaintiff's claim is for £5,000[1], being the price of work done and materials supplied by the Plaintiff for and at the request of the Defendant at 10 Ironside Villas, Upton, Somerset in or about June 1981.

PARTICULARS

Demolishing existing coal bunker	500.00
Construct new 5′ × 3′ × 4′ coal bunker in fair faced brick	2,500.00
Supply and fix 'Blackamore' coal bunker cover	2,000.00
	£5,000.00

AND THE PLAINTIFF CLAIMS

(i) £5,000

*   (ii) Interest thereon pursuant to statute.[2]

Precedent 2
Statement of Claim for payment under quantum meruit
by reference to invoice; part paid

The Plaintiff's claim is for £4,000,[1] being the balance of the price of work done and materials supplied by the Plaintiff for and at the request of the Defendant at 10 Ironside Villas, Upton, Somerset in or about June 1981.

PARTICULARS

Invoice No 9987 dated 1st August 1981, full particulars of which have been delivered to the Defendant on or about 2nd August 1981[3]	5,000.00
Less	
Paid by the Defendant on or about 15th August 1981	1,000.00
Balance outstanding	£4,000.00

AND THE PLAINTIFF CLAIMS

(i) £4,000.00

*   (ii) Interest pursuant to statute.[2]

Precedent 3
Statement of Claim for payment under informal lump-sum
contract with extra work

1 By a contract between the Plaintiff as Contractor and the Defendant as Employer the Plaintiff agreed to execute and the Defendant agreed to pay for certain building work at 10 Ironside Villas, Upton, Somerset. The terms of the said contract are contained in, alternatively evidenced by, the Plaintiff's letter to the Defendant of 1st June 1981.

2 The agreed price for the said work was £5,000.00

3 The Plaintiff has duly executed the said work together with certain further work ordered by the Defendant to a value of £3,000.00. The total sum due to the Plaintiff under the said contract is accordingly £8,000.00, particulars of which appear by the Plain-

tiff's invoice No 9987 dated 1st August 1981 delivered to the Defendant on or about 2nd August 1981.[3]

4 The Defendant has failed to pay the whole or any part of the said sum of £8,000.00

AND THE PLAINTIFF CLAIMS

(i) £8,000.00

(ii) Interest pursuant to statute.[2]   *

Precedent 4
Statement of Claim for payment under an interim
architect's certificate

1 By contract in writing dated 1st June 1981 between the Plaintiff as Contractor and the Defendant as Employer, the Plaintiff agreed for the consideration therein mentioned to carry out certain building works at 10 Ironside Villas, Upton, Somerset. The said contract was in the Standard Form of the Joint Contract Tribunal, Private Edition, With Quantities, 1980 Edition.

2 There was an express term, inter alia, by clause 30.1.1 of the said Contract that the Architect should from time to time issue Interim Certificates stating the amount due to the Plaintiff from the Defendant and that the Plaintiff should be entitled to payment therefore within 14 days from the date of issue[4] of each Interim Certificate.

3 Pursuant to the said term the Architect named in the said Contract, L da Vinci, issued Interim Certificate No 2 on 15th August 1981 in the sum of £5,000.

4 The Defendants have failed to honour the Certificate within 14 days or at all

AND THE PLAINTIFF CLAIMS:

(i) £5,000

(ii) Interest pursuant to Statute.[2]   *

Notes to precedents

1 Dates, sums and other numbers must be expressed in a pleading in figures and not in words (Ord 18, r 6(3)).

2 Following the introduction of Ord 22, r 1(8) (payments into Court   * now include such interest as might be awarded under the Law Reform (Miscellaneous Provisions) Act 1934, s 3), the editors of the *White Book Supplement* now suggest that it would seem desirable, if not necessary, expressly to include a claim for interest

if interest is sought, notwithstanding *Riches* v *Westminster Bank Limited* [1943] 2 All ER 725 (see the *Supplement's* notes at 22/1/6).

3 Where it is necessary to give particulars of debt, expenses or damages and those particulars exceed three folios, they must be set out in a separate document referred to in the pleading and the pleading must state whether the document has already been served and, if so, when or is to be served with the pleading (Ord 18, r 12(2)). 'Folio' means seventy-two words, each figure being counted as one word (Ord 1, r 4(1)).

4 Under Clause 30(1) of the 1963 Private Editions of the JCT Contract, interim certificates were payable within fourteen days from the *presentation* of the certificate by the contractor to the employer. Consequently, it was appropriate to also plead the fact and time of presentation.

* 1 Financing charges

Increasing attention has been focused over the last few years upon the question of interest. Under the Law Reform (Miscellaneous Provisions) Act 1934 the court has power to award interest upon a judgment, but that Act forbids the award of interest upon interest (compound interest) and it does not apply to allow a plaintiff in litigation to obtain interest where a debt is paid late but before the issue of proceedings.

In *F G Minter Limited* v *Welsh Technical Services Organisation* (1980) 13 BLR 1 the Court of Appeal vindicated the principle that interest may be recoverable as loss and/or expense under the express terms of a building contract, and in *Techno-Impex* v *Gebr van Weelde Scheepvaartkantoor BV* [1981] Com LR 82), Lord Denning held that it is open to arbitrators in the City of London to award interest by way of damages where the claimants had suffered loss by being kept out of their money. In this case, Lord Denning expressly said that this principle applies where the principal sum is paid before the commencement of the arbitration and interest is claimed for the period of delay. In that case, a shipping case, the principal claim was for demurrage, and the court was, therefore, expressly sanctioning the award of interest upon interest since, although interest upon interest was forbidden by the 1934 Act, arbitrations are not subject to it.

Where interest is being claimed not under the 1934 Act but as damages for breach of contract or loss and expense, it is now common to refer to it as finance charges, or financing charges.

In the case of small claims where it is intended to proceed under Ord 14 there is little material advantage in pleading financing charges. In a more substantial case, however, where substantial delay is anticipated, then it is always worthwhile to consider making a claim for financing charges.

2 Particulars

Where a case is destined for the Official Referee's court, the Official Referee will, in an appropriate case, order the preparation of a Scott Schedule (see p 124). In these circumstances there is often little point in the parties giving or requiring further and better particulars in the ordinary form where to do so would lead only to duplication.

Where a plaintiff knows that he will have to give extensive particulars, for example on a lengthy claim for extra work or in respect of many defects, it is often convenient for him to particularise these matters by an appendix to his statement of claim in a form that can itself be used as a Scott Schedule. By doing this, he can save time and avoid duplication.

That said, it is often of great importance to obtain proper particulars of an opponent's pleading under Ord 18, 12. In particular, it is quite common for a claim on a lump-sum contract not to give particulars as to how the sum claimed is to be reconciled with the pre-agreed lump sum or as to the basis of each and every item of the extra work. It will rarely advantage an opponent to wait until trial before pointing to the inadequacy of such a pleading, and provided it is properly timed an interlocutory attack upon such a pleading, which usually involves seeking those particulars, can have devastating effects. Likewise, a party making a claim in respect of defects in negligence frequently particularises the defects complained of but not the negligence relied upon. Being required to particularise that negligence can often give such a party cause for doubt as to his prospects of success.

Notice to admit facts

Notices to admit facts are certainly of value in assisting a party to know what facts he is expected to prove at trial and what facts are not seriously in dispute. In practical terms, however, the notice to admit facts is probably even more valuable as a means of encouraging settlement. Order 27 r 2(1) provides as follows:

> 'A party to a cause or matter may not later than 21 days after the cause or matter is set down for trial serve on any other party a notice requiring him to admit, for the purpose of that cause or matter only, the facts specified in the notice.

Notices to admit facts are often very lengthy, and set out to dissect issues of fact into individual parts. It is a feature of the present pleading system that a party can plead his case generally, and thereby reach an advanced stage in litigation without applying his mind to the question of precisely which facts he is going to be able to prove or resist in evidence at trial. In practice, notices to admit facts are capable of being used to good effect in a rhetorical way as well as in a genuinely inquisitorial way.

Chapter 13
Discovery and Inspection of Documents

The same principles as to discovery and inspection of documents apply in building contract matters as in other litigation and arbitration, and the extensive notes to Ord 24 are as helpful as always.

Under Ord 24, r 2, the parties must exchange lists of documents within fourteen days after the close of pleading. In practice, this rule is frequently disregarded, and in many cases where the documentation is heavy compliance with it would be entirely impracticable. The Official Referees do not usually expect discovery to have taken place when the matter first comes before them, and orders for discovery are usually made at that stage.

In arbitrations, an order for discovery is usually made at the preliminary meeting, and the typical form of order for directions, given in *The architect as arbitrator*, contains the following precedent:

> 'That after the close of pleading the Claimant and Respondent do respectively within . . . days deliver to the other a list of the documents which are or have been in their possession or power relating to the matters in question in this arbitration and that inspection be given within . . . days thereafter.'

Where the documentation is heavy, it is frequently impracticable to list each and every document, and the parties resort to bundling (see Ord 24 r 5(1) and the note at 24/5/4). Where the litigation involves particularly contentious issues it is normal to list individually the documents relating specifically to those issues, and to list by bundles the other documents. Where documents are listed by bundles particular care must obviously be taken to ensure that documents are not removed from the bundles, and it is often appropriate for each page of the discovered documents to be separately marked with a mechanical numbering machine, a process that is much quicker than page-by-page description in a list of documents. When this is done the parties sometimes reach an arrangement whereby, for example, the plaintiff uses numbers from 1 to 499,999 and the defendant uses the numbers from 500,000 onwards.

It is sometimes said that building contract litigation can be won or lost at discovery. It is certainly the case that it is very common for a party not to disclose all the documents that it ought to disclose at discovery, and much can hinge upon the steps taken by that party's opponent to obtain all the documents. The documentation obviously varies from case to case, but the following comments are frequently of relevance.

1 Reports upon the defects and third-party correspondence

Frequently, a party obtains a report upon defects in the work soon after they appear and before litigation is contemplated. Those reports are only privileged from production if the purpose of preparing for litigation is either the sole reason for the preparation of the report, or at least the dominant purpose of it (*Waugh* v *British Railways Board* [1979] 3 WLR 150 HL.

In the case of a dispute between an employer and a contractor as to defects, there will often be correspondence between the employer and the architect. This correspondence is sometimes marked 'without prejudice'. Unless that correspondence falls within the privilege rules enunciated in *Waugh* v *British Railways Board*, it will generally be discoverable to the contractor.

Likewise, in the case of a dispute between the employer and the contractor, correspondence between the contractor and the sub-contractor upon the defects is usually discoverable to the employer, and in the case of a dispute between a contractor and a sub-contractor as to defects, correspondence as to the defects between the employer and the contractor is usually discoverable to the sub-contractor.

2 Architect's documents

It is usually thought that an employer has the right to delivery up of the architect's plans and other documents, at any rate unless the architect has a lien on them for non-payment of fees (see *Hudson*, p 188). Accordingly, the architect's documents are usually regarded as within the power of the employer, and therefore discoverable by the employer in litigation between the employer and the contractor.

In the case of litigation between the employer and the architect, the employer is entitled to his usual rights of discovery against the architect notwithstanding the existence of a lien on the documents (*Woodworth* v *Conroy* [1976] QB 884).

3 Contractor's documentation

In the case of a dispute between the employer and the contractor as to payment for the works, the employer will frequently be entitled to see at discovery many documents that he has not seen before.

Most contractors keep prime-cost records, often on computer. This is so even in the case of lump-sum contracts where the contractor is not entitled to be paid the prime cost of the works as such: the records are kept by the contractor inter alia so that eventually he can see whether he has made a profit on the contract or not. In all but the simplest cases, these prime-cost records do relate to the issues in question, and are discoverable by the contractor to the employer. Contractors usually keep a site diary on site containing contemporaneous notes as to the works, and this site diary is usually discoverable.

Where the contractor makes a claim for a profit element on works he has undertaken, or where the Hudson formula is relevant (see p 43), the employer can sometimes press for discovery of the contractor's profit and loss accounts since these documents will disclose the profit usually earned by the contractor.

4 Sub-contractor documentation

Where a dispute arises between the employer and the contractor as to payment, the employer will often be entitled to discovery of all correspondence and other documentation passing between the contractor and the sub-contractor. The employer is not, however, usually entitled to discovery of the sub-contractor's own documentation since this is not usually within the power of the contractor.

Chapter 14
Expert Evidence

It is particularly common for expert evidence to be necessary in building contract litigation.

The purpose of expert evidence is as to fact and not as to law. Accordingly, expert evidence is not generally appropriate to assist the court to construe the terms of the contract, nor is it appropriate to adduce expert evidence as to whether a particular head of claim is admissible. These are matters of law, and however unfamiliar they may be to a general practitioner lawyer it is the function of the lawyers and not of the expert witnesses to unravel the terms and effect of the contract.

Expert evidence can, however, be indispensable both for the purpose of ascertaining what sum is due to the contractor, and for the purpose of establishing the responsibility for, and extent of, building defects.

1 Expert evidence upon payment for the works

There are various matters upon which expert evidence may be appropriate in this area.

First, disputes sometimes arise as to whether work undertaken by a contractor is properly to be regarded as extra work or whether it is properly to be regarded as being within the scope of the work originally undertaken by the contractor. Where there are formal bills of quantities, those bills of quantities are usually to be interpreted in accordance with the Standard Method of Measurement. The JCT contract expressly so provides in Clause 2.2.2.1, and even if there is no express provision a similar effect may be incorporated by implication. In some cases, it can be appropriate to adduce expert evidence as to whether a description in the bills of quantities is sufficient to include all the work actually carried out by the contractor.

It is comparatively rare for a building contract dispute to turn upon the quantity of work actually carried out by the contractor. Where such a dispute does arise it can be appropriate to adduce expert evidence upon this.

More commonly, disputes arise as to the rate of payment to which the contractor is entitled. Such disputes arise not only with regard to the whole contract works where the contract is for a reasonable sum, but also with regard to the valuation of extra work. In some cases, much of the evidence at trial consists of the experts for both sides being taken through a lengthy Scott Schedule and expressing views upon the value of many items of work.

Where there are defects in the works the contractor can sometimes fall into the trap of adducing evidence as to the defects without adducing evidence as to the credit to be given to the contractor in respect of work that he has done which does not require replacement.

In all these cases, the person best able to give the expert evidence is usually a quantity surveyor, although in small cases the evidence of an architect or building surveyor may suffice.

2 Expert evidence as to defects

There are three main issues in this area where expert evidence is frequently necessary:

(i) Is there a defect in the works?
(ii) If so, whose responsibility is that defect? (This issue frequently turns upon whether the defect arises out of a design fault or bad workmanship.)
(iii) Where the obligation of the person responsible for the defect is not an absolute one but merely an obligation to use proper skill and care, did that person exercise proper skill and care?

It is not uncommon for a plaintiff to be able to satisfy the court as to issues (i) and (ii) above but to fail to adduce proper evidence in respect of (iii). In some cases, this oversight can be fatal. In *Worboys* v *Acme Investments Ltd* (1969) 4 BLR 133, Sachs LJ had this to say:

'To my mind the architect's duty was limited to one of showing reasonable competence in an attempt to produce saleable houses at around the price which the defendants had in mind.

Now Mr Harvey urges that this is a class of case in which the court can find a breach of professional duty without having before it the standard type of evidence as to what constitutes lack of care on the part of a professional man in the relevant circumstances. There may well be cases in which it would not be necessary to adduce such evidence – as, for instance, if an architect omitted to provide a front door to the premises. But it would be grossly unfair to architects if, on a point of the type now under consideration, which relates to a special type of dwelling, the courts could without the normal evidence condemn a professional man. . . . In those circumstances I have come to the conclusion that there was simply no evidence that there was any breach of duty on the part of the plaintiff in this instance.'

It is, therefore, highly desirable that a plaintiff should form a realistic assessment as soon as possible as to whether or not the defendant's obligation is absolute or whether he must show negligence. If negligence is an indispensable part of his claim, the sooner he obtains expert evidence upon that issue the better. It is entirely unreliable for the plaintiff to hope for assistance from the doctrine res ipsa loquitor.

3 The rules as to expert evidence

The rules as to expert evidence in civil proceedings were substantially changed following the Civil Evidence Act 1972 and now appear in Ord 38, Pt IV, beginning at Ord 38, r 35.

The function of expert witnesses is (inter alia) to explain words, or terms of science or art appearing on the documents which have to be construed by the court, to give expert assistance to the court (eg as to the laws of science, or the working of a technical process or system), or to inform the court as to the state of public knowledge with regard to the matters before it (see *Crosfield & Sons Ltd* v *Techno-Chemical Laboratories Ltd* (1913) 29 TLR 379; *British Celanese Ltd* v *Courtaulds Ltd* (1935) 152 LT 537 HL). In building contract cases expert evidence is not infrequently used in relation to such matters as the reasons for the failure of a building, the factual matters necessary to determine whether a particular failure was negligent and the practice of the building industry with regard to various matters such as the practices embodied in the Standard Method Measurement. It is not open to parties to give expert evidence as to matters of English law, and accordingly expert evidence is not used to assist the court as to the construction of contracts.

The restrictions on adducing expert evidence appear at Ord 38, r 36, which provides as follows:

'36—(1) Except with the leave of the Court or where all parties agree, no expert evidence may be adduced at the trial or hearing of any cause or matter unless the party seeking to adduce the evidence has applied to the Court to determine whether a direction should be given under r. 37, 38 or 41 (which ever is appropriate) and has complied with any direction given on the application.

(2) Nothing in paragraph (1) shall apply to evidence which is permitted to be given by affidavit or shall affect the enforcement under any other provision of these Rules (except Ord 45, r. 5) of a direction given under this Part of this Order.'

It is apparent from the terms of Ord 38, r 36, that a party seeking to adduce expert evidence must, unless he obtains the leave of the court or the agreement of all parties, not only obtain a direction as to that evidence, but must also comply with that direction.

Order 38, r 37, deals with medical evidence in action for personal injuries.

Order 38, r 38, applies to expert evidence in other actions, and is the rule usually applicable in building contract litigation.

Order 38, r 41, relates to expert evidence of engineers in motor accident cases.

Order 38, r 38, provides as follows:

38.—(1) Where an application is made under rule 36 (1) in respect of oral expert evidence to which rule 37 does not apply, the Court may, if satisfied that it is desirable to do so, direct that the substance of any expert evidence which is to be adduced by any party be disclosed in the form of a written report or reports to such parties and within such period as the Court may specify.

(2) In deciding whether to give a direction under paragraph (1) the Court shall have regard to all the circumstances and may, to such an extent as it thinks fit, treat any of the following circumstances as affording a sufficient reason for not giving such a direction:

(*a*) that the expert evidence is or will be based to any material extent upon a version of the facts in dispute between the parties; or

(*b*) that the expert evidence is or will be based to any material extent upon facts which are neither:

(i) ascertainable by the exercise of his own powers of observation, nor

(ii) within his general professional knowledge and experience.'

The whole purpose of Ord 38 is, in relation to expert evidence, to save expense by dispensing with the calling of experts where there is in reality no dispute and, where there is a dispute, by avoiding parties being taken by surprise as to the true nature of the dispute and thereby being obliged to seek amendments or adjournments; and in either case, probably lead to the settlement of the action. Therefore, the court should in practice ordinarily make an order for the exchange of non-medical expert reports (*Ollett* v *Bristol Aerojet Limited* (practice note) (1979) 1 WLR 1197).

The ordinary practice of the Official Referee's Court is to consider with the parties the need for expert evidence on the first occasion that the matter comes before the Official Referee. In theory, the onus of satisfying the court to give a direction for the disclosure of expert evidence is upon the party applying for such disclosure to be made, but in practice the onus is not a heavy one (*White Book* paragraph 38/37–39/8). The court does not usually give one party the right to call expert evidence without giving a similar right to the other party; the court usually directs that the parties simultaneously exchange their experts report on or before a fixed date, which is usually some months before the trial date. The court sometimes directs that the experts reports be agreed if possible. The court also has power under Ord 38, r 4, to limit the number of expert witnesses who may be called at trial.

Where a party fails to apply for or comply with a direction of the court to adduce expert evidence at trial, he runs the risk that evidence will be excluded at trial. Parties are often a few days late in complying with an exchange date contained in a direction and provided that this is well before trial no harm is caused. The court tends to take a more serious view where an experts report is not delivered until the month of trial, or where a party seeks to adduce evidence materially outside the terms of the report previously delivered. Sometimes, a party is penalised in costs; for example, where a defendant failed to serve on the plaintiff the report of his expert in breach of Ord 38, r 40, but nevertheless, in spite of its imperative terms, obtained the leave of the trial judge to admit the report under the powers conferred by the opening words of r 36 (1), he was awarded his costs taxed up to the date of the hearing, but only half the costs of the trial of the action (*Cable* v *Dallatinca* (1977) 12 ST 705).

By Ord 38, r 39, the court has power to direct that a part only of expert evidence sought to be adduced should be disclosed, and by Ord 38, r 44, the court has power to revoke or vary a previous direction as to expert evidence.

Expert evidence is normally only given on affidavit on interlocutory hearings, and at trial a party adducing disputed expert evidence is normally expected to call that expert so as to give the other party the opportunity of cross-examination.

The court has a further power under Ord 40 to appoint a court expert, but only rarely avails itself of this power.

In arbitrations, the arbitrator does in practice enjoy considerable latitude in the control of proceedings (*Star International* v *Bergbau-Handel* [1966] 2 Lloyd's Rep 16); but he is bound to follow as closely as possible the procedure adopted by the courts. In many cases, the arbitrator will have been chosen by reason of his own specialist knowledge, and may therefore be less reliant upon expert evidence than a court would be.

4 The payment of experts

A solicitor instructing an expert on behalf of a client should make it plain whether he does so as principal or agent. Unless he makes it plain to the expert that it is the client who is responsible for the payment of fees, the solicitor may have a responsibility to pay them. The solicitor's responsibility may arise not only in contract but also as a matter of professional conduct. The Law Society's *A Guide to the Professional Conduct of Solicitors* gives the following guidance at chapter 6, paragraph 9:1:

'In all cases where a solicitor has not clearly disclaimed personal liability to pay witnesses and other persons advising him in their professional capacity, he is obliged to pay them their proper fees and accordingly failure to do so will amount to unbefitting conduct which may lead to disciplinary action.'

For the purposes of taxation of party and party costs, both the fees of expert witnesses and the costs of solicitor and counsel in obtaining and considering their reports or advice are recoverable in a proper case. The court has an over-riding discretion regarding costs, however, and *Cable* v *Dallatinca* (1977) 121 SJ 705 illustrates the power of the court to penalise the party in costs in an appropriate case. In *F Rigolli* v *Lambeth* (5 December 1977) (unreported) Donaldson J sitting with assessors held that the Taxing Master was wrong to disallow the costs incurred in calling a second expert witness as this was in his view unnecessary. If a witness was called the cost involved should not be disallowed unless the judge so ordered.

Chapter 15
Dismissal for Want of Prosecution

There are various rules of the Supreme Court which empower the court to dismiss an action for want of prosecution: Ord 19, r 1 (where the plaintiff is in default of service of Statement of Claim); Ord 24, r 16(1) (default in the discovery and production of documents); Ord 25, r 1(4) (default in taking out a Summons for Directions); Ord 26, r 6(1) (default in answer to interrogatories); and Ord 34, r 2 (default in setting down). In addition, the court has an inherent jurisdiction to dismiss an action for want of prosecution where there is default in compliance with an order of the court or where the plaintiff is guilty of excessive delay in the prosecution of the action.

In *Birkett* v *James* [1977] 3 WLR 38 the House of Lords reviewed the principles upon which the jurisdiction of the court to dismiss an action for want of prosecution is exercised. Lord Diplock said that

'the power should be exercised only where the court is satisfied either
(1)   that the default has been intentional and contumelious, e.g., disobedience to a peremptory order of the court or conduct amounting to an abuse of the process of the court; or
(2)   (a)   that there has been inordinate and inexcusable delay on the part of the plaintiff or his lawyers, and
       (b)   that such delay will give rise to a substantial risk that it is not possible to have a fair trial of the issues in the action or is such as is likely to cause or to have caused serious prejudice to the defendants either as between themselves and the plaintiff or between each other or between them and the third party.'

The application of these rules to building contract litigation is of especial importance because of the great difficulty that plaintiffs frequently have in adhering to the time scale set out in the rules of the Supreme Court.

The cases upon dismissal for want of prosecution are reviewed in the notes to the *White Book* at Para 25/1/3A et seq. There are three cases that are of particular importance to building contract cases: *Renown Investments (Holdings) Limited* v *F Shepherd & Son* (1976) 120 SJ 840, *Birkett* v *James* [1977] 3 WLR 38 and *Bremer Vulkan* v *South India Shipping* [1981] 2 All ER 289.

142

1 Renown Investments v Shepherd

The flood of applications by defendants for dismissal for want of prosecution began in the late 1960s. After a few years the Court of Appeal heard *Renown Investments (Holdings) Limited* v *F Shepherd & Son* (1976) 120 SJ 840. In that case the plaintiff claimed damages for breach of contract and for an alleged negligence against contractors, engineers and architects arising out of building defects. The pleadings were closed in December 1971 and by July 1974, when there had been no summons for directions and no discovery, the defendants issued a summons to strike out the action for want of prosecution.

It was urged for the plaintiff that building contracts were so complicated and detailed that they are in a special category so that a great deal of time can be spent in preparing them for litigation. The court rejected that contention and held that building contract litigation is not in any special category and should be prosecuted expeditiously in compliance with the RSC time scale, particularly where it involves charges of negligence against professional men.

2 Birkett v James

In *Birkett* v *James* [1977] 3 WLR 38 the House of Lords has put two very important limits upon the power of the court to dismiss actions for want of prosecution.

First, the power will not usually be exercised where the limitation period has yet to expire. Lord Diplock said:

> 'For my part, for reasons that I have already stated, I am of opinion that the fact that the limitation period has not yet expired must always be a matter of great weight in determining whether to exercise the discretion to dismiss an action for want of prosecution where no question of contumelious default on the part of the plaintiff is involved; and in cases where it is likely that if the action were dismissed the plaintiff would avail himself of his legal right to issue a fresh writ, the non-expiry of the limitation period is generally a conclusive reason for not dismissing the action that is already pending.'

The second limit relates to the time which elapses before the issue of a writ. It had been settled law even before *Birkett* v *James* that a plaintiff who left it until the last moment before issuing a writ was in greater danger of being struck out. In the words of Lord Diplock:

> 'A late start makes it all the more encumbent upon the plaintiff to proceed with all due speed and a pace which might have been excusable if the action had been started sooner may be inexcusable in the light of the time that has already passed before the writ was issued.'

However, in order to justify dismissal of an action for want of prosecution, the House of Lords in *Birkett* v *James* held that the defendant must, if he is to succeed, point to delay which the plaintiff allows to elapse unnecessarily *after* the writ has been issued, and must further show that delay in prosecuting the action after that time has added to the prejudice which the defendant would have sustained in any event from the late issue of the writ. The additional prejudice need not be great compared with that which may have been caused by the time elapsed before the writ was issued, but it must be more than minimal.

* 3 Bremer Vulkan v South India Shipping

For a brief adventurous moment, the Court of Appeal in *Bremer Vulkan* v *South India Shipping Corporation* [1981] 2 All ER 289 held that similar principles to those set out in *Birkett* v *James* also applied to arbitration, either because the High Court has an inherent jurisdiction to control proceedings before arbitrators or because failure by the plaintiff to avoid inordinate and inexcusable delay could represent a repudiatory breach of an implied term in the arbitration agreement. The House of Lords has, however, overruled this decision (22 January 1981); and it now appears that the only remedy of a respondent where the claimant is guilty of delay is to press for an early hearing date.

4 Practice

It is very common for building contract litigation to take a long time, and a plaintiff is often quite unable to adhere to the time scale laid down by the rules of the Supreme Court for taking various steps. A plaintiff's real risk begins once six (or twelve) years have passed since the date of the accrual of the cause of action.

Of course, the safest course for a plaintiff is to pursue the litigation as rapidly as possible. Where, however, it is not possible for the plaintiff to take any particular step within the time laid down by the rules, he should obtain an extension of time either by agreement or from the court. Where, for example, the plaintiff wishes to postpone a hearing or to defer the fixing of a hearing so that without prejudice discussions may take place, then he should obtain the agreement of the defendant to that postponement. An agreement between the parties that the hearing should be adjourned generally with leave to restore when both parties are ready or an agreement to the like effect will preclude the defendant from applying to strike out for want of prosecution without at any rate giving reasonable notice of his own readiness and requiring the opposite party to be ready (*Banca Popolare di Novara* v *John*

Livanos & Sons Ltd (1973) 117 SJ 509). If a plaintiff is in genuine difficulties in meeting the time-limit, and cannot obtain an extension from the defendant, he may apply to the court for an extension of time, and the court has power to extend the period within which a plaintiff is required to do any act in any proceedings (Ord 3, r 5(1)).

There is no prescribed stage at which the defendant may apply to the court to exercise its inherent jurisdiction to dismiss a plaintiff's action for want of prosecution. Sometimes, the defendant will issue his summons upon receipt of notice of intention to proceed under Ord 3, r 6. Sometimes, the application will be coupled with an application for or following an 'unless' order.

In support of his application, the defendant will almost always need an affidavit in support, and the affidavit must generally show three things:

  (i) that the limitation period has expired;

  (ii) that there has been inordinate and inexcusable delay since the date of the issue of the writ, referring particularly to any delay immediately preceding the issue of the summons; and

  (iii) that the defendant has suffered some real prejudice by reason of that delay. (Examples of prejudice are that the memories of the main witnesses will have faded, or that witnesses have died or left the employ of the defendant and cannot be traced, or that the passage of time has rendered it impossible or difficult to obtain necessary evidence from an inspection of the building in question. Prejudice may sometimes be caused by the loss of opportunity to pursue remedies against third parties, although the proper time for issuing third party notices is prior to the service of the defence and it may be necessary to show exceptional circumstances (such as the intervening insolvency of a third party) in order to show prejudice.)

Ordinarily, the plaintiff should file an affidavit in reply endeavouring to explain all the circumstances relied upon as excusing the delay and, where appropriate, making proper comment upon the prejudice referred to in the defendant's affidavit.

Chapter 16
Arbitration

* Arbitration arises out of a written agreement to submit present or future differences to arbitration, whether an arbitrator is named therein or not (Arbitration Act 1950, s 32). That is to say, it arises as a matter of contract. It is, however, a contract that is much affected by the provisions of the Arbitration Acts and by common law.

It is a mistake to think of arbitration as an option open to save the trouble of litigation. Arbitration is akin to litigation there the parties have chosen their own judge (or a means of appointing their own judge). There are usually pleadings, interlocutory applications, discovery, inspection, briefs, witnesses, subpoenas, trials, taxation of costs and appeals, and the arbitrator is bound to reach his decision according to the legal rights of the parties and not according to what he may consider fair and reasonable under all the circumstances (*Taylor (David) & Son Ltd* v *Barnett Trading Co* (1953) 1 WLR 562, 568).

There are three relevant Arbitration Acts:

(a) *The Arbitration Act 1950*—This Act was a consolidation of the previous law and sets out the main body of arbitration law. An annotated version appears at para 3703 et seq of Part 2 of the 1979 *White Book.*

(b) *The Arbitration Act 1975*—This Act deals with arbitrations with a foreign element. Section 1 removes the court's discretion to stay court proceedings. For claims within a non-domestic arbitration agreement, the court *must* now stay such court proceedings. Sections 2 to 6 give effect to the New York convention on the Recognition and Enforcement of Foreign Arbitral Awards. The Act is printed with notes at para 3822 et seq of Part 2 of the 1979 *White Book.*

(c) *The Arbitration Act 1979*—This Act replaces s 21 of the 1950 Act (which provided for appeal by way of case stated) with a new appeals procedure and a new procedure for taking preliminary points in the High Court. By s 5 it also provides for the High Court to empower an arbitrator to make 'unless' orders. It is printed at para 3835 et seq of the supplement to the 1979 *White Book.*

146

As to the procedure in arbitration, there is no comprehensive set of rules comparable to the rules of the Supreme Court, the Matrimonial Causes rules or the County Court rules. The Arbitration Act 1950 contains what are in effect a number of terms to be implied into the arbitration agreement but these do not condescend to great detail.

For this reason, the conduct of arbitration tends to be at times haphazard in comparison with court proceedings. The standard work on arbitration is *Russell on Arbitration* (A Walton, Ed, 19th ed; Stevens and Son Ltd, 1979). In practice, arbitrations conducted before experienced arbitrators are generally conducted according to established customs which are set out with admirable clarity in the RIBA publication *The architect as arbitrator*. The 1978 edition is available from RIBA Publications Ltd, 66 Portland Place, London, W1N 4AD at a cost of £2.00 (or £2.30 including postage) and runs to 72 pages. This edition was prepared by LWM Alexander BArch, FRIBA, FRICS, PPIArb together with Norman Royce FRIBA, PPIArb and AB Waters CBE, GM, FRIBA, FRIAS, PPIArb, all of whom are senior arbitrators. This book is much to be recommended but it does not deal with the Arbitration Act 1979 and should be read in conjunction with it.

This chapter deals only with arbitration pursuant to arbitration clauses in building contracts. In particular, it does not relate to arbitrations under statutes, nor does it relate to arbitrations within the meaning of the County Court rules.

1 The arbitration notice

The term 'arbitration notice' is usually used to describe the notice from one party to a contract requiring the other party to agree to submit a dispute between them to an arbitrator. Its significance arises out of the Limitation Act 1980, for under s 34 of that Act it is the service of an arbitration notice that is regarded as the commencement of the arbitration for limitation purposes, and thus equivalent to the issue of a writ in the High Court for that purpose. It should be noted that although the arbitration notice marks the commencement of the arbitration for limitation purposes, it does not represent the commencement of the arbitration in any other sense, and an arbitration is not regarded as having been commenced until such time as an arbitrator has accepted a proper appointment.

An arbitration notice need not be in any prescribed form, and it is usual for it simply to contain a notice of dispute and a request of the other party to concur in the appointment of an arbitrator. The terms of the notice generally depend upon the terms of the arbitration clause in the contract relied upon. A typical wording of an arbitration notice written by a solicitor where the contract is in the standard JCT form is as follows:

Dear Sirs,

We are instructed by Messrs Blank in relation to their contract with you for works at Blank.

We hereby give you notice on behalf of our clients of disputes or differences that have arisen between you and them and hereby request that you concur in the appointment of an arbitrator.

Yours faithfully,

It is usually unwise to try to particularise the nature of the dispute in the notice to concur.

An arbitration notice is not usually regarded as an offer capable of acceptance, nor does it operate to activate any arbitration machinery. The arbitration does not commence until an arbitrator is actually appointed. Further, there is nothing to prevent a claimant from serving an arbitration notice before, at the same time as or after issuing a writ in the court. However, the service of an arbitration notice by a party who is already a plaintiff is frequently regarded as adding fuel to the fire of a defendant who takes out a Section 4 summons to stay any parallel proceedings in the court. For this reason, it is common practice in appropriate cases to make the position entirely plain in the arbitration notice, by adding a further paragraph along the following lines:

'Please take note that our clients take the view that the proper forum for the hearing of this dispute is the High Court. This notice is accordingly served in order to protect our clients' position for limitation purposes.'

It is sometimes said that this paragraph should be contained in a separate letter dispatched contemporaneously with the arbitration notice, but it is open to doubt whether this procedure carries with it any advantage. In any event, doubts have been expressed as to whether such a paragraph deprives the arbitration notice of its effect for limitation purposes but notwithstanding those doubts it probably represents the best available course in an unsatisfactory area of law.

Arbitration notices are sometimes typed up as formal legal documents with words like 'In the matter of the Arbitration Act 1950' at the top of the page. There is no harm in this practice but a letter is quite sufficient.

2 Choosing an arbitrator

The arbitration clause in the JCT form of contract (Article 5) provides that the arbitrator shall be a person agreed between the parties to act as arbitrator, or failing agreement within fourteen days after the arbitration notice, a person to be appointed on the request of either party by the president or the vice president for the time being of the Royal Institute of British Architects. Forms of contract published by other professional bodies generally provide for appointment by their own president for the time being failing agreement by the parties. Some other forms of building contract simply provide that disputes shall be referred to arbitration without providing the machinery for selection of an arbitrator where the parties cannot agree; in such a case the High Court has power to appoint an arbitrator under the Arbitration Act 1950, s 10.

The question arises how should a party select an arbitrator whom he seeks to have appointed? This is a matter of experience and knowledge of the many names to choose from, but it is possible to give certain guidelines:

(a) in the case of substantial disputes where the sum in dispute exceeds say £100,000, then it is normal to appoint one of the few senior building contract arbitrators in the country. There is no substitute for the personal experience of these men in making a choice between them. In any event, great caution should be exercised before appointing an arbitrator who is not a member of the Institute of Arbitrators.

(b) Specialist counsel generally know by reputation if not by personal experience of arbitrators who habitually arbitrate in building contract disputes.

It is not normal to seek the consent of a proposed arbitrator before suggesting his name to the other party. The suggestion is generally made subject to that arbitrator consenting to act.

When suggesting the arbitrator to the other party, it is frequent practice to suggest two names. Often the party making the suggestion will put his first choice second in the belief that the second-placed suggestion is more likely to be acceptable than the first.

It goes without saying that to attempt to have appointed an arbitrator who is not or may not be impartial is a recipe for disaster. It does no harm, however, when considering the other party's proposals as to choice of arbitrator, to ask for warranties that the proposed arbitrator does not have, so far as the other party is aware, any interest or potential interest in the dispute or connection with the parties.

3 The appointment of the arbitrator

Where the parties are able to agree upon a suitable arbitrator, one or the other of them should write to the proposed arbitrator asking whether he is prepared to accept the appointment. It is customary to enclose copies of the correspondence following the arbitration notice and wise to ask for details of the remuneration that the arbitrator will require. The arbitrator's authority does not commence until he has accepted the appointment.

Even before the appointment of the arbitrator it is customary to follow the normal rules as to communications with the arbitrator as follows:

(a) neither party should exchange any verbal communication with the proposed arbitrator except in the presence of the other party;

(b) telephone messages should only be relayed through the arbitrator's secretary; and

(c) each party should immediately send a copy of any written communication with the arbitrator to the other party.

Where it is not possible to agree the proposed arbitrator with the other party, it is necessary to apply to the RIBA or other professional body, or to the court.

To obtain the appointment of an arbitrator by the RIBA it is necessary to write to the RIBA at 66 Portland Place, London, W1N 4AD, requesting a form of application. The RIBA will then provide a standard form of application for appointment which requires to be executed by one or both of the parties. One or both of the parties is required (jointly and severally) to agree as follows:

(i) to provide adequate security for the due payment of the fees and expenses of the arbitrator if he so requires;

(ii) to pay the fees and expenses of the arbitrator whether the arbitration reaches a hearing or not; and

(iii) to take up the award (if any) within ten days within receipt of notice of publication.

Arbitrations frequently involve a claimant who is keen to proceed with the arbitration and a respondent who is considerably less keen. Sometimes the respondent declines to sign the application form. The RIBA will not appoint an arbitrator unless the claimant himself signs and returns the form, thus making himself primarily liable to provide any required security and to pay the arbitrator's fees and expenses. What can the claimant do? It is plain from the Arbitration Act 1950, s 12(1), that it is an implied term of arbitration agreements that each party will do all things required by the arbitrator for the proper conduct of the arbitration but it is not clear what effect the section has before the arbitrator is actually appointed. In theory it might perhaps be possible to obtain an injunction requiring the respondent to execute the form of appointment, but in practice this is likely to be unrealistic and the claimant must choose between himself accepting responsibility for the arbitrator's fees and expenses or instituting or returning to proceedings in the court. A defendant who has refused to execute the standard RIBA form of appointment may well have difficulty in showing that he is and remains ready and willing to do all things necessary to the proper conduct of the arbitration, as he would be required to show under the Arbitration Act 1950, s 4.

The standard RIBA form of appointment contains a space for the signed acceptance of the appointed arbitrator.

Where there is no machinery for appointment by the president of a professional body and it is necessary to apply to the court under the Arbitration Act 1950, s 10, then application is made to the High Court by originating summons (Ord 73, r 3).

4 The preliminary meeting

It is customarily the arbitrator's first step upon appointment to call the parties to a preliminary meeting, which is analogous to an immediate summons for directions. It is suggested in *The architect as arbitrator* that the directions may be given in a form which sets out a time-table for the delivery of pleadings, a time-table for discovery, for agreement of figures etc, as to the number of experts, that communications to the arbitrator should be simultaneously copied to the other party, and as to costs and liberty to apply.

It is normal for the parties to be represented at the preliminary meeting by their solicitors, although representation is sometimes by counsel in large cases.

It is customary (but by no means universal) for the arbitrator to be handed the original contract at the preliminary meeting.

5 Interlocutory matters

In practice, arbitrators in building contract matters follow High Court procedure as closely as possible, with the exception that arbitrators do not usually strike out pleadings or dismiss a claimant's claim for want of prosecution (*South India Shipping* v *Bremmer Vulkan* [1981] 2 All ER 289).

In respect of arbitrations commenced after 1 August 1979, the position has been materially altered by the Arbitration Act 1979, s 5(1) and (2), which provide as follows:

'**5**—(1) If any party to a reference under an arbitration agreement fails within the time specified in the order or, if no time is so specified, within a reasonable time, to comply with an order made by the arbitrator or umpire in the course of the reference, then, on the application of the arbitrator or umpire or of any party to the reference, the High Court may make an order extending the powers of the arbitrator or umpire as mentioned in subsection (2) below.

(2) If an order is made by the High Court under this section, the arbitrator or umpire shall have the power, to the extent and subject to any conditions specified in that order, to continue with the reference in default of appearance or of any other act by one of the parties in like manner as a judge of the High Court might continue with proceedings in that Court where a party fails to comply with an order of that court or a requirement of the rules of court.'

The practical effect of s 5 is that where necessary the High Court may clothe the arbitrator with the power to make 'unless' orders.

In the case of arbitration commenced before 1 August 1979, or where the arbitrator is unduly hesitant in the exercise of his powers, the High Court has power to make direct orders under the Arbitration Act 1950, s 2(6), which provides as follows:

'(6) The High Court shall have, for the purpose of and in relation to a reference, the same power of making orders in respect of—

(a)   security for costs;

(b)   discovery of documents and interrogatories;

(c)   the giving of evidence by affidavit;

(d)   examination on oath of any witness before an officer of the High Court or any other person, and the issue of a commission or request for the examination of a witness out of the jurisdiction;

(e)   the preservation, interim custody or sale of any goods which are the subject matter of the reference;

(f)   securing the amount in dispute in the reference;

(g)   the detention, preservation or inspection of any property or thing which is the subject of the reference or as to which any question may arise therein, and authorising for any of the purposes aforesaid any persons to enter upon or enter into any land or building in the possession of any party to the reference, or authorising any samples to be taken or any observation to be made or experiment to be tried which may be necessary or expedient for the purpose of obtaining full information or evidence; and

(h)   interim injunctions or the appointment of a receiver; as it has for the purpose of and in relation to an action or matter in the High Court;

Provided that nothing in this subsection shall be taken to prejudice any power which may be vested in an arbitrator or umpire of making orders with respect to any of the matters aforesaid.'

6 Sealed offers

There is no formal procedure in arbitrations equivalent to payment into court, and accordingly there has evolved the practice of making sealed offers in appropriate cases. The following very helpful guidance appears in *The architect as arbitrator*:

'In arbitrations such an offer is made in writing, a copy of the letter being placed in a sealed envelope and handed to the arbitrator for him to open after he has made his award, but before he comes to consider the question of costs. In this way the arbitrator is not hampered in arriving at his decision as to what ought to be paid by knowing what has been offered.

The arbitrator may find the very existence of a "sealed offer" from one of the parties to be slightly prejudicial to his consideration of the amount to be awarded as it can be interpreted as an admission of some liability. This disadvantage can be overcome by agreeing with both the parties at the outset (without them disclosing which of them would be making the offer) that the arbitrator will issue an interim award after the hearing dealing finally with the subject matter in dispute but reserving his decision on costs to his final award. After the publication of the interim award, the arbitrator can hear submissions from the parties on the question of costs when the existence of any open offer to settle can be announced and the liability for costs adjusted accordingly.'

7 Trial

Unless many people need to be present, interlocutory hearings in arbitrations are very frequently held at the offices of the arbitrator. It is usually necessary, however, to hire a room for the trial itself, and it is frequently left to the solicitors for the parties to perform this function.

In some arbitrations it is regarded as desirable to have a transcript record of the proceedings, which can be done by shorthand writers or mechanical recording. Again, it is usually left to the parties' solicitors to arrange this if appropriate.

In major building contract litigation the proceedings at trial are scarcely distinguishable from trial in the courts, save that the advocates do not appear robed and the arbitrator is addressed as 'Sir' rather than 'Your Honour' or 'My Lord'. The usual rules apply as to evidence, and the court has powers under the Arbitration Act 1950, s 12, to make orders with regard to subpoenas and such matters.

It should not be forgotten that a Bible is necessary to swear in the witnesses.

8 Appeals

The rules as to appealing from the decision of arbitrators were radically changed by the Arbitration Act 1979, ss 1–4. Before that Act came into force the position was governed by the rules of the Arbitration Act 1950, s 2, as to the statement of cases by arbitrators for a decision of the High Court, which were widely regarded as unsatisfactory.

If an appeal is contemplated then reference must be made to the terms of the Arbitration Act 1979, but in any event it is important to have regard to the Arbitration Act 1979, s 1(6)(*a*); if a party contemplates the possibility of an appeal he should give notice to the arbitrator that a reasoned award is required.

Under the Arbitration Act 1979, s 2, the High Court now has power to determine any question of law arising in the course of the reference in an appropriate case. The section replaces the previously unsatisfactory position whereby preliminary points of law, if to be tried before the court, had to be tried by way of case stated upon a preliminary point.

9 The ICC Court of Arbitration

The International Chamber of Commerce Court of Arbitration has been in existence for more than fifty years, and is established as the major international 'independent' arbitration service. Compared with domestic arbitrations, international arbitrations are necessarily expensive and troublesome. In practical terms, that is inevitable and in major contracts between parties resident in different countries (particularly where one party is a government) arbitration before the ICC Court of Arbitration represents the only acceptable means of resolving disputes since only the ICC Court of Arbitration can offer a sufficient guarantee of neutrality.

In the building contract world, international contracts are frequently entered into in the FIDIC form, which is prepared by the Fédération Internationale Des Ingénieurs-Conseils, and is in effect an adaptation from the ICE form of contract. The FIDIC contract contains an arbitration clause referring disputes which cannot be settled by the engineer to the ICC Court of Arbitration.

Where the ICC Court of Arbitration has been nominated in the arbitration agreement, it is unlikely that the arbitration agreement will be a 'domestic arbitration agreement' within the meaning of the Arbitration Act 1975. In the case of a non-domestic arbitration agreement, the court does not have a *discretion* under the Arbitration Act 1950, s 4, to stay any proceedings commenced in the court. It *must* stay the court proceedings under the Arbitration Act 1975, s 1(1), which provides as follows:

'**1**—(1) If any party to an arbitration agreement to which this section applies, or any person claiming through or under him, commences any legal proceedings in any Court against any other party to the agreement, or any person claiming through or under him, in respect of any matter agreed to be referred, any party to the proceedings may at any time after appearance, and before delivering any pleadings or taking any other steps in the proceedings, apply to the Court to stay the proceedings; and the Court, unless satisfied that the arbitration agreement is null and void, inoperative or incapable of being performed or that there is not in fact any dispute between the parties with regard to the matter agreed to be referred, shall make an Order staying the proceedings.'

It can be seen that although the court does not have its discretion in non-domestic cases, there are three circumstances where the court will allow court proceedings to continue.

(1) Where the defendant takes a step in the proceedings, which he may do by accident or design (see p 111).

(2) Where the court is satisfied that the arbitration agreement is null and void, which will usually hinge upon whether the whole of the contract is null and void.

(3) It will be seen that the Arbitration Act 1975 expressly preserves the principle enunciated in *Ellis Mechanical Services Ltd v Wates Construction Limited* (1976) 2 BLR 60; that is to say, that it is for the court to decide whether or not there is a dispute. It seems that the words of Lord Denning MR in that case at p 61 are applicable in non-domestic cases as well as in domestic cases:

'The defendants cannot insist on the whole going to arbitration by simply saying that there is a difference or dispute about it. If the court sees that there is a sum which is indisputably due, then the court can give judgment for that sum and let the rest go to arbitration . . .'

Indeed, this passage was cited by Geoffrey Lane LJ in *Associated Bulk Carriers* v *Koch Shipping* (1977) 7 BLR 18, a case decided under the Arbitration Act 1975. In that case, the *Ellis* case was distinguished upon the ground that, although liability was admitted by the defendants and it was clear that the plaintiffs would recover substantial damages, there was no definable or quantified part of the plaintiffs' claim which was not in fact in dispute. The defendants were able to avoid an Ord 14 judgment by putting up various different calculations as to the minimum sum due. All the judges in the case found that the defendants were devoid of any merits, and were seeking arbitration in order to take advantage of the long delays involved in arbitration. Although it does not appear from the judgment, it may be that the conclusion to be drawn from *Associated Bulk Carriers* v *Koch Shipping* is that the court adopts a more cautious and less robust approach to Ord 14 cases where there is a non-domestic arbitration agreement than it does where there is a domestic one.

Even if one of the above three circumstances appertain, an English claimant is likely to have other difficulties apart from the Arbitration Act 1975 which he must overcome in order to proceed in the English courts. If he wishes to serve the proceedings upon a defendant outside the jurisdiction, he must obtain the ex parte leave of the court under Ord 11, r 1. If the court grants leave to serve the writ out of the jurisdiction, the defendant can apply to set aside the writ on the ground of want of jurisdiction under Ord 12, r 8.

Where the claimant does not wish or cannot have the matter dealt with by the English courts, then he will generally serve his opponent with a formal arbitration notice for limitation purposes, and then approach the International Chamber of Commerce.

The head office of the International Chamber of Commerce is at 38 Cours Albert-1er, 75008 Paris. The British National Committee of the ICC has offices at Centre Point, 103 New Oxford Street, London WC1A 1QB (tel 01-240 5558) and it is possible to obtain from that address the thirty-two page booklet which sets out the Rules for the ICC Court of Arbitration. The Rules provide for pleadings, submission of all relevant documents, hearings, amendments and costs. The Rules also contain a scale of administrative expenses and fees as from 1 March 1980, which is as follows:

'To calculate the administrative expenses and the fee, the percentages applied to each successive slice of the sum in dispute are to be added together.

(a) Administrative expenses

Sum in dispute			Administrative Expenses
Under	50,000 (in US Dollars)		4.00% (min $1,000)
From	50,001 to	100,000	3.00%
From	100,001 to	500,000	1.50%
From	500,001 to	1,000,000	1.00%
From	1,000,001 to	2,000,000	0.50%
From	2,000,001 to	5,000,000	0.20%
From	5,000,001 to	10,000,000	0.10%
From	10,000,001 to	50,000,000	0.05%
From	50,000,001 to	100,000,000	0.02%
Over	100,000,000		0.01%

(b) Arbitrator's fees

Sum in dispute			Fees	
			Minimum	Maximum
Under	50,000 (in US Dollars)			$1,000
From	50,001 to	100,000	1.50%	6.00%
From	100,001 to	500,000	0.80%	3.00%
From	500,001 to	1,000,000	0.50%	2.00%
From	1,000,001 to	2,000,000	0.30%	1.50%
From	2,000,001 to	5,000,000	0.20%	0.60%
From	5,000,001 to	10,000,000	0.10%	0.30%
From	10,000,001 to	50,000,000	0.05%	0.15%
From	50,000,001 to	100,000,000	0.02%	0.10%
Over	100,000,000		0.01%	0.05%'

Accordingly, in a case where the sum claimed is, say, $120,000 the administrative expenses and arbitrator's fees payable will fall in the range $5,710 to $8,400. In addition to these expenses and fees, the parties must pay the expenses, if any, of the arbitrator and the fees and expenses of any experts. The court may depart from these scales in exceptional circumstances. The costs of the arbitration must be paid before a case can be submitted to the arbitrator, and if the respondent cannot be persuaded to contribute, the claimant may have to pay the full amount in advance himself. In addition, the costs of the parties themselves likely to be incurred in conducting an arbitration abroad are inevitably higher than the costs of domestic arbitration or litigation.

In addition to the Court of Arbitration, the ICC has its own Administrative Commission for Conciliation.

Chapter 17
Limitation of Actions

* The law as to limitation of actions in building contract matters has changed out of recognition in the last ten years with the huge extension of the law of tort in this area. Limitation in building contract cases is now extremely complex and in many respects is a matter of conjecture. It is beyond the scope of this book to review the law of limitation in any detail. The comments that follow are far from exhaustive, and are intended to represent the broad direction of the law rather than a full and accurate analysis of it.

An employer's action in contract against a contractor for defects generally becomes statute-barred about six years after the date when the contractor was obliged to complete the works. If the contract was under seal, the period is twelve years. In the case of contracts where there is an express defects liability period, it is sometimes said that the employer's action in contract becomes statute-barred six (or twelve) years from the expiry of the defects liability period. This rule is subject to the important exception under the Limitation Act 1980, s 32, under which the limitation period can be extended if the contractor has concealed the defect by 'fraud'. This section is now construed widely in building contract cases and may apply even where the employer had the benefit of agents overseeing the works (*Lewisham Borough Council* v *Leslie & Co* (1979) 250 EG 1289).

In an employer's action in negligence against a builder for defects, the claim becomes statute-barred six years from the date on which the cause of action accrued (Limitation Act 1980 s 2). Differing views have been expressed as to when the cause of action accrues. In *Sparham Souter* v *Town & Country Development (Essex) Ltd* [1976] QB 858 the Court of Appeal said:

> 'Time does not begin to run until such time as the plaintiff discovers that [the defective work] has done damage, or ought, with reasonable diligence to have discovered it.'

In practice, the limitation period for the purpose of an action in tort can be much longer than the limitation period for an action in contract, especially since it appears that every new owner of the

158

building may acquire a new and distinct cause of action and hence a new and distinct limitation period (*Sparham Souter* v *Town & Country Development (Essex) Limited* [1976] QB 858).

In a contractor's action in contract against a subcontractor in respect of defects, the position appears to depend upon whether the subcontract contains an express clause indemnifying the contractor against breaches of contract. If so, the contractor's action upon the indemnity clause is not statute-barred until six (or twelve) years from the date when the liability of the main contractor to the employer has been established (*County and District Properties* v *Jenner* [1976] 2 Lloyd's Rep 728).

In the case of a claim under the Defective Premises Act 1972, the claim becomes statute-barred six years after the time when the dwelling was completed or when remedial work was finished (Defective Premises Act 1972, s 1(5)).

Special rules apply to claims for contributions under the Law Reform (Married Women and Tortfeasers) Act 1935 or the Civil Liability (Contribution) Act 1978.

A contractor's claim against an employer for payment frequently becomes statute-barred piecemeal. Much depends upon the precise terms of the contract but sometimes the first parts of the claim will become statute-barred six years after the commencement of work and the last part of the claim will become statute-barred about seven years after the completion of the work.

For the purpose of proceedings in the High Court, the action will be statute-barred unless the plaintiff has issued his writ within the limitation period. For the purposes of arbitration proceedings, an action is statute-barred unless the claimant has, within the limitation period, served upon the respondent a notice requiring the respondent to concur in the appointment of an arbitrator (Limitation Act 1980, s 34). There is no provision whereby a plaintiff in the High Court can rely upon the date of an arbitration notice, nor any provision whereby a claimant in an arbitration can rely upon the date of the issue of a writ. Unless and until a party knows with certainty which forum the dispute will be heard in, his only safe course in order to stop time running is both to issue a writ and serve an arbitration notice.

Chapter 18
Settlement

The vast majority of building contract cases are settled. Because of the complexity and cost of bringing a building action to trial the settlement rate is probably higher than in other High Court actions.

Some commercial lawyers and general practitioners take the view that litigation or arbitration is the end of the line. If they fail to achieve a commercial settlement without proceedings, they sometimes assume that they can delegate the file for the purpose of the interlocutory stages, and then instruct eminent leading counsel for the trial. This attitude is based upon the premise that the case will go to trial. But it is far more likely that the case will be settled, and the terms of settlement are usually very heavily influenced by the interlocutory process. For this reason, the raison d'être of many interlocutory steps in well-conducted building contract litigation is often to improve the climate for settlement, as well as to prepare for trial.

To achieve the best possible climate for settlement, a party's main objective is to diminish his opponent's expectation of success at trial. This point has many practical effects. In particular, a party may have a choice as to whether or not to stress to his opponent a particular difficulty that his opponent would have at trial. To hold one's fire until trial may have the advantage of a surprise element at trial. To stress those points in correspondence before trial may have the advantage of diminishing one's opponent's expectation of success. Usually, the second advantage is of more importance since the case is more likely to be settled than to go to trial.

Achieving the climate for settlement

By their nature building contract disputes often involve many issues. Some of those issues will usually assist one party and others assist the other. An experienced litigator will select those issues that highlight his opponent's weaknesses, and at interlocutory stages he will seek to fight upon those issues. If he can, he will rely upon them in his Ord 14 affidavit or to show that his opponent has disclosed no course of action, or he will take them as a preliminary point or concentrate on them at discovery.

160

Sometimes, a party can find two or three issues upon which he can base interlocutory applications. If that party can achieve two or three successes upon interlocutory hearings, that can achieve for him an extremely good climate for settlement. If his opponent sees himself worsted on two or three issues in a row, he is unlikely to be consoled by the thought that there are another dozen issues to go.

The best time for settlement depends upon the particular circumstances of the case. For a plaintiff this often occurs shortly after obtaining an Ord 14 judgment for part of the claim; for a defendant, it is often when the plaintiff's task of preparing for trial appears to be most long and difficult, which is often part way through the discovery process.

It is comparatively rare for correspondence between the parties' solicitors during the course of the litigation to be referred to at trial, a fortiori, if the correspondence is marked 'without prejudice'. The inter-solicitor correspondence can, however, have a marked effect upon the climate for settlement. A party can often improve the chances of a favourable settlement by repeatedly making unanswerable rhetorical points, even if those points relate to comparatively minor issues. The correspondence can further be of importance in keeping the door open for settlement discussions. It is not necessarily a sign of weakness for a party to suggest settlement; for example, where a defendant sued for £100,000 suggests settlement at £1,000, that suggestion is a sign of strength and not of weakness and yet can force the plaintiff to think in terms of what settlement might be possible.

It sometimes happens that a party does what seems to be necessary to achieve a suitable climate for settlement and yet the other party still appears inclined to pursue the case. In those circumstances it can sometimes tip the balance to write a long 'without prejudice' letter which recites all the unanswerable points in extenso, however minor. The letter then goes on along the following lines:

> 'In view of all the above matters, we fail to see how your client can enjoy any great prospect of success at trial. We are accordingly instructed to make an offer of settlement as follows . . .
>
> 'If, however, you take the view that we are mistaken as to any of the above points, then we invite you to put forward your reasons in writing. If those reasons are valid, then we will advise our client to improve the above offer.'

That letter should be used with some caution, for to put forward bad or answerable points may damage the position rather than improve it.

Where there are matters of fact which assist, then it is often desirable to set out those matters of fact in a notice to admit facts under Ord 27, r 2 (1), which provides as follows:

'A party to a cause or matter may not later than 21 days after the cause or matter is set down for trial serve on any other party a notice requiring him to admit, for the purpose of that cause or matter only, the facts specified in the notice.'

If a party is served with a notice to admit facts, and neglects to admit a fact which ought properly to have been admitted, he will ordinarily be ordered to pay the other party's costs of proving that fact regardless of the result of trial as a whole. Accordingly, a notice to admit facts can force a party to consider what facts are certain to be proved against him, and this can have a material effect upon the climate for settlement. It is surprisingly common for a party not to settle only because he has not properly considered the strength of the case against him.

1 Without prejudice funding agreements

There is a special case where it is sometimes appropriate to reach a partial settlement.

Defects sometimes appear in building work that the employer alleges are the responsibility of the contractor. The contractor denies that they are his responsibility but both the employer and contractor are at one that there are defects and that the employer will suffer a substantial loss if the defects are not rectified without delay. In those circumstances it can be in the interests of both the employer and the contractor to reach a without prejudice funding agreement. The terms of such an agreement are usually along the following lines:

(1) The contractor agrees that, without prejudice to the question of his liability to do so, he will execute the necessary remedial work;

(2) The employer agrees on a cash flow basis to pay x% of the cost of the remedial work, such payment to be made without any set off except arising out of the remedial work itself, and

(3) It is agreed that both the employer and the contractor have the right to refer the question of liability to litigation or arbitration, and in particular the employer is entitled to claim repayment of the sum paid by him, and the contractor is entitled to claim the balance of the cost (plus a reasonable percentage for profit) of the remedial works.

Such an agreement is not usually regarded as without prejudice in the sense of a without prejudice offer since it represents a concluded agreement (*Tomlin* v *Standard Telephones & Cables Limited* [1969] 1 WLR 1378). Accordingly, the agreement may be referred to in court, but the court is not to regard the agreement as tantamount to an admission of liability for the defects by either side.

It is good practice expressly to exclude the employer's right of set off against his obligation to make the funding payment. The exclusion may well be implied if not expressed but it should be made clear that the employer is not permitted to enter into a without prejudice funding agreement, have the remedial work done, and then refuse to pay the agreed percentage upon the ground that he thinks the defects were the contractor's responsibility anyway.

The time of making a without prejudice funding agreement is, of course, also the time to consider whether to appoint an expert to inspect the work before the physical evidence of the defects is lost for all time.

2 Risk formula calculation

Much litigation in the High Court concerns a single issue. As soon as the parties have a feel for the strength of their respective cases, they have a feel as to the area within which they look for settlement.

Building contract litigation frequently involves a multiplicity of claims. The parties often have a feel about the respective strengths and weaknesses of these claims but that does not of itself provide a feel for the area of settlement. A calculation is sometimes necessary for this purpose.

It is rarely possible to be entirely confident of any claim in a building action. There is usually a risk that the claim will not succeed. In crude terms, the claim can be valued by applying its percentage prospect of success to the sum in issue.

Take a simple example. Suppose a contractor sues an employer for £60,000. Of this, £10,000 relates to payment for the work which has been certified by the architect and the balance of £50,000 is a claim for loss and expense which the architect has not certified. Of this, £30,000 is a prolongation claim and £20,000 is a disruption claim. By way of set-off the employer brings a claim against the contractor for £215,000, of which £15,000 relates to clearly visible defects and £200,000 relates to a speculative claim that the foundations are defective. The parties can crudely calculate the settlement area by valuing these claims and cross-claims as follows:

	Sum Claimed	Percentage Prospect	Value of Claim
Contractor's claim:			
Certified sums	10,000	90%	9,000
Loss and Expense			
Prolongation	30,000	70%	21,000
Disruption	20,000	40%	8,000
			38,000
Employer's claim:			
Patent defects	15,000	80%	12,000
Foundations	200,000	5%	10,000
			22,000
Balance:			
Value of contractor's claim			38,000
Less			
Value of Employer's claim			22,000
BALANCE			16,000

By means of a risk formula calculation such as this, the parties might accordingly come to the view that a reasonable settlement might be for the employer to pay the contractor £16,000. If either party feels that it is in a strong position in the litigation, it can aim for a more ambitious settlement. Risk formula calculations can be very sophisticated, and take into account costs orders already made, cost orders liable to be made, irrecoverable party and party cost element, interest and so on. However sophisticated they are, they should, however, be seen with circumspection. The result is as likely to prove correct at trial as a family is to have 0.95 children.

3 Terms of settlement

In general terms, the same considerations apply to the settlement of building contract cases as other litigation. There are, however, one or two matters worthy of comment.

It is usually dangerous to relate the terms of settlement to the particular contract since parallel causes of action may exist in tort, in quasi-contract, or under a collateral contract. Accordingly, the terms of settlement frequently include wording along the following lines:

'. . . in full and final settlement of all the plaintiff's claims of whatsoever nature (including without prejudice to the generality of the foregoing all future claims, costs and interest) against the defendant relating to or connected with the works executed by the plaintiff/defendant at . . . on or about. . . .'

Care should be given to whether the terms of settlement include future actions. It is clear from *Sparham-Souter* v *Town & Country Developments (Essex) Limited* [1976] 1 QB 858 that for the purpose of an action in negligence no cause of action arises unless and until the plaintiff can show some actual injury. Accordingly, unless the settlement refers to future claims, it may not operate to settle a claim by an employer in negligence in respect of defects where no actual injury had been suffered at the time of the settlement.

Sometimes a settlement is intended to be a compromise of only certain defects, and is not intended to compromise the employer's rights in respect of other defects which have yet to appear. If that is the intention, particular care needs to be exercised because there is authority in *Conquer* v *Boot* [1928] 2 KB 336 to the effect that in a claim for defects in an ordinary lump-sum contract there is only one cause of action in contract in respect of all the defects. Accordingly, the terms of settlement should specify with particularity which defects are within the scope of the settlement, and care should be taken before consenting to any court order embodying the terms of settlement lest future claims should become res judicata.

Where the claim being settled is a claim by a contractor in respect of which the architect has not issued certificates, it may be appropriate in the terms of settlement to preclude the contractor from bringing any subsequent claim against the architect in negligence for undercertification.

Where a case is settled between the employer and the contractor, and there remain outstanding claims by or against subcontractors, then great care needs to be taken in the terms of settlement. There is particular difficulty where the subcontract contains a pay-when-paid clause or where the subcontractor's entitlement is related to architects' certificates, as under NSC/4. It is a matter of great uncertainty what effect a settlement between an employer and a contractor has upon the sub-contractor in such circumstances, and the terms of settlement sometimes contain elaborate provisions including indemnity clauses.

In the settlement of defect claims, it is now perhaps appropriate for the building owner to indemnify the contractor or other claimee against any subsequent claim by any subsequent building owner (see *Sparham-Souter* v *Town & Country Developments (Essex) Ltd* [1976] 1 QB 858).

Chapter 19
The Law

Building contract law is overwhelmingly common law. The standard books on the law of contract and the law of tort are of some assistance but for a description of building contract law in any detail it is necessary to look at the specialist text books.

An excellent work on building contract law appears in volume 4 of the fourth edition of *Halsbury's Laws of England* by Keith Goodfellow (whose death was a great loss to the Bar), John Blackburn and Anthony Thornton.

The leading book on building contract law is usually regarded as being *Hudson's Building and Engineering Contracts* (10th edition by I N Duncan Wallace QC; Sweet & Maxwell Limited 1970; 1979 Supplement).

Great authority is also attached to *Building Contracts* by Donald Keating QC (4th edition 1978, Sweet & Maxwell Limited). This book contains a very helpful commentary upon the 1977 Revision of the 1963 edition of the JCT Standard Form, and many of these comments are equally applicable to the corresponding provisions in the 1980 edition of the Contract. It also contains a commentary by John Uff on the 1973 Fifth Edition of the ICE form of Contract. John Uff is also the author of a shorter work, *Construction Law* (3rd edition 1981, Sweet and Maxwell Limited).

There are several publications which consist of an analysis of the building contract standard forms. In particular, the following by I N Duncan Wallace QC, published by Sweet & Maxwell Limited: *Building & Civil Engineering Standard Forms* (1969), which contains a commentary upon the 1963 edition of the JCT Contract and must be read in conjunction with the 1970 and 1973 Supplements; *The ICE Conditions of Contract* (5th edition 1974, 1980 Supplement); *Further Building and Engineering Standard Forms* (1973); and *the International Civil Engineering Contract* (1974, 1980 Supplement).

The law of tort in building matters has developed with enormous speed over the last few years and there is no authoritative text-book dealing specifically with this very important area of law. Some of the more important cases in this area are as follows:

Anns v *Merton Borough Council* [1978] AC 728

Batty v *Metropolitan Property Realisation Ltd* [1978] QB 554

B L Holdings Ltd v *Robert J Wood & Partners* [1979] 12 BLR 1

Dutton v *Bognor Regis Urban District Council* [1972] 1 QB 373

Independent Broadcasting Authority v *EMI Ltd & BIC* [1981] 14 BLR 1

Sparham-Souter v *Town and Country Development (Essex) Ltd* [1976] 1 AB 858

Sutcliffe v *Thackrah* [1974] AC 727

All these cases are reported in *Building Law Reports*, currently edited by Humphrey Lloyd QC and Colin Reese.

Glossary

Actual cost. This expression is sometimes used as a synonym for prime cost in a cost contract; see p 3.

- **Adjudicator.** Creature of Clause 24 of the JCT nominated sub-contract form NSC/4 (formerly clause 13B of the Green Form), an adjudicator is like an 'instant arbitrator' for the purpose of quantifying the contractor's set-off against a nominated sub-contractor. The adjudicator is appointed by agreement between the contractor and the sub-contractor, and is usually a quantity surveyor.

Application. This usually means an application by a contractor or sub-contractor for interim payment or for reimbursement of loss and expense eg under Clause 26.1 of the JCT contract.

- **Arbitrator.** (i) Generally, a person qualified to act as arbitrator, often an architect but sometimes an engineer, quantity surveyor or a barrister. Membership of the Institute of Arbitrators is common but not essential.

(*ii*) In particular, a person appointed as arbitrator pursuant to an arbitration agreement within the meaning of the Arbitration Act 1950.

- **Architect.** (*i*) Generally, a person entitled to practise or carry on business under any name, style or title containing the word 'architect', being registered in the Register of Architects; Architects Registration Act 1938, s 1(1). In broad terms, this means someone with the initials RIBA after his name.

(*ii*) In particular, the architect with the contractual status under a contract to issue instructions and certificates as to various matters. He may or may not have designed the works; his function is to exercise control over the works as they proceed. Used loosely in this sense, 'architect' can sometimes include any engineer, surveyor or supervising officer with this contractual function.

Articles of agreement. Usually means the articles of agreement which are to be found in the opening pages of the JCT contract.

Artists and tradesmen. Expression used in the old JCT contract to mean persons who execute work not forming part of the main contract. The expression was dropped in the 1980 edition.

Bill of quantities. A full description of the amount of work necessary for completion of building works. In major projects, there are likely to be several volumes, and the bills will respectively deal with such matters as preliminaries, foundations, framework etc. Bills of quantities have columns on the right hand side of the page to allow the contractor to price the work. *The Standard Method Measurement of Building Works*, 6th Edition, published by the Royal Institution of Chartered Surveyors and the National Federation of Building Trades Employers sets out rules for the preparation and interpretation of Bills of Quantities.

Bill of variations. An account prepared at the end of the contract showing the effect upon the pre-agreed lump sum of variations to the works.

Bills. Shorthand for bills of quantities

Bondsman. Synonym for the surety (eg under the ICE Form of Performance Bond). Often a bank or insurance company.

Buggeration. Builders' jargon for disruption. Sometimes used loosely to include prolongation.

Building employer. Synonym for employer.

Building inspector. Local authority officer charged with ensuring compliance with Building Regulations.

Building owner. This expression is sometimes used as a synonym for the employer.

Building surveyor. This expression is sometimes used to describe a surveyor in general practice, in contrast to a quantity surveyor.

Certifier. The person named in a contract as having power to issue certificates which have a contractual effect. In the JCT contract the certifier is either the architect (Private editions) or the supervising officer (Local Authorities editions). In the ICE contract the certifier is the engineer.

Claims consultant. A quasi-professional person who carries on the business of drafting, negotiating and advising upon claims for the payment of money or extension of time under building contracts. Usually a quantity surveyor by training.

Clerk of Works. An appointee of the employer whose duty is to act as an on-site inspector. His powers to give instructions to the contractor are usually limited. Usually a builder by training.

Client. Synonym for employer.

Completion. The completion of the execution of the work.

Completion date. In JCT form of contract (1980 edition), the originally agreed date for completion as extended by the architect.

Consortium. In the building industry, this expression most commonly means a partnership between two or more contractors which subsists for the purpose of one project only. The expression is also sometimes used to describe a joint venture between contractors, whether or not that joint venture is strictly speaking a partnership in the legal sense of the word.

Contract. In addition to its legal meaning, this expression is often used to describe the project as a whole.

Contract sum. This expression is generally used to describe the pre-agreed price for lump sum building works. In the JCT contract it has a particular definition which excludes VAT. The expression is not usually used to describe the sum that the contractor is entitled to at the end of the day; this is called the 'adjusted contract sum' in Clause 30.6.3 of the JCT contract.

Cost contract. A contract where the contractor's final entitlement is calculated by reference to the actual cost of the works, rather than by reference to a pre-agreed lump sum. See p 2.

Cost plus contract. Synonym for cost contract.

Cost plus percentage contract. Synonym for cost contract.

CPA conditions. The model conditions for the hiring of plant of the Contractors' Plant Association. See p 12.

Critical delay. A delay that causes or contributes towards a delay in completion of building works as a whole. See p 62.

CVI. Confirmation of Verbal Instruction, ie the confirmation by the contractor in writing of a verbal instruction of the architect (eg under Clause 4.3.2. of the JCT contract).

Date for completion. In JCT form of contract, the date by which the contractor must complete if his time is not extended. Cf completion date.

Defects liability period. A 'guarantee' period from practical completion within which the contractor must remedy any defects appearing in the works without charge. The expression has a particular definition under Clause 1.3 of the JCT contract.

Delay. Sometimes means delay in the completion of the works that is the responsibility of the contractor.

Disruption. Loss and expense caused to a contractor by reason of breaches or failures by the employer or his agents that do not necessarily result in prolongation of the works as a whole.

Domestic subcontractor. A subcontractor other than a nominated subcontractor.

Employer. A person who enters into a contract with a building contractor whereby he angages to pay for building works. The expression is not usually used to include the employing party to a sub-contract.

Engineer. (*i*) Generally , a professionally qualified civil engineer, structural engineer, heating and mechanical engineer, etc.
(*ii*) In particular, the person so named in an ICE or FIDIC contract.

Entire completion. Completion in every respect, exceptionally a condition precedent to payment. See p 2.

Estimator. A person employed by a contractor to estimate the cost of proposed building works.

Expert. (*i*) A person who gives expert evidence in litigation or arbitration.
(*ii*) The expression is sometimes used to describe a person who decides some matter between two parties, but whose position is not that of an arbitrator within the meaning of the Arbitration Act 1950.

Extended preliminaries. Method of calculation of a contractor's on-site losses following prolongation. Widely thought to be fallacious. See p 42.

Extras. Synonym for extra work, that is to say extra work required to be carried out by the employer, or the architect on behalf of the employer, not included within the original contract work.

Final account. The calculation of the sum due to the contractor in respect of the contract as a whole. The expression is used as a shorthand for the 'computation of the adjusted Contract Sum for the Works', referred to in Clause 30.6.3 of the JCT contract.

- **Financing charges.** (*i*) Where the cost of being left out of money is claimed, not as interest on a debt, but as a constituent part of the debt it is now fashionable to refer to it as financing charges, or finance charges, following the language used in *FG Minter* v *Welsh HTSO* (1980) 13 BLR1. See p 43.
  (*ii*) less delicately, synonym for interest.
  (*iii*) the expression is sometimes used to refer particularly to delay in the release of retention money.

Fluctuations. Adjustments to a contract sum that fall to be made by reason of increases or decreases in the cost of the works. See p 36.

Foreman-in-charge. Designation in the old JCT Form of the contractor's on-site representative.

Formula rules. The formula rules issued by the Joint Contracts Tribunal for use with Clause 40 of the JCT contract, which is one of the alternative fluctuation clauses.

General contractor. Demodé synonym for main contractor.

Green form. The form of sub-contract for use where the sub-contractor is nominated under the 1963 edition of the JCT Form issued under the sanction of and approved by the National Federation of Building Trades Employers and the Federation of Association of Specialists and Sub-contractors and approved by the Committee of Associations of Specialist Engineering Contractors. Now supplanted by NSC/4 or NSC/4(a).

Hancock v Brazier terms. The three terms usually implied in a contract for the sale of a house to be erected. See p 30.

Hudson formula. Method of calculating a contractor's loss of gross profit following prolongation. See p 43.

ICE. The Institution of Civil Engineers.

JCT. The Joint Contracts Tribunal. See p 6.

Joiner. A carpenter, usually responsible for finer work.

- **Labour-only subcontractor.** In theory, a sub-contractor who enters into sub-contracts for the provision of labour but not materials. In practice, a workman taxed under Schedule D.

List of rates. Usually, the pre-agreed rates in a re-measurement contract.

Lump sum. The pre-agreed consideration in a lump-sum contract.

Lump sum contract. A contract to execute work for a pre-agreed lump sum. See p 1.

Maintenance period. Synonym for defects liability period.

Management contractor. (*i*) A party which does not undertake any part of the works itself, but which contracts with the employer to act as an organiser of other contractors.

(*ii*) A contractor who undertakes works, usually on a cost plus basis, with the intention of sub-contracting the whole of the works.

Measurement. Usually means the measurement of the amount of building work done.

Measurement and value contract. Synonym for re-measurement contract.

Minor works agreement. The Agreement for Minor Building Works issued by the JCT. See p 14.

Nominated Sub-Contractor. Generally, a sub-contractor with whom a main contractor enters into contract pursuant to the instructions of the architect. The expression has a precise meaning in JCT contracts (at Clause 35.1 of the 1980 edition; a different definition appeared at Clause 27(a) of the 1963 edition).

Official Referee. For practical purposes, one of the three judges who hear building contract cases in the High Court. In theory, the post was abolished by the Courts Act 1971 and the function formerly exercised by the Official Referee is now exercised by designated circuit judges. See p 118.

Official referee's schedule. A form of pleading commonly used in the Official Referee's Court, where the contentions of the parties appear in tabular form. See p 124.

Omissions. Items of original contract work required not to be carried out by the employer or the architect on the employer's behalf.

Operative. Synonym for workman.

Package deal contract. Synonym for design and build contract.

Pay-when-paid clause. A clause in a sub-contract which provides that the main contractor need not pay the sub-contractor until the main contractor himself receives payment from the employer in respect of those works.

Performance bond. This expression has various meanings. In the building industry it does not usually mean the kind of 'on demand' banker's bond which stands on a similar footing to a letter of credit; *Edward Owen Engineering Ltd* v *Barclays Bank International Ltd* [1977] 1 WLR 764. It usually means a guarantee in the ordinary sense of the word by a surety, often a bank or insurance company, that the contractor will perform his obligations under the contract.

Performance specification. A specification which defines the physical characteristics required of building works, eg the air temperature to be attained by a central heating system given an ambient temperature or the rate of air change to be attained by a ventilation system.

Period of final measurement. The period referred to in Clause 30.6.1.2 of the JCT contract within which the quantity surveyor must prepare and deliver a statement of all the final valuations of extra work etc.

Person-in-charge. JCT jargon for foreman-in-charge.

Plant. (*i*) Equipment such as cranes, earthmoving equipment, generators, and other equipment used in the execution of building works.
(*ii*) Machinery installed in a finished building.

Practical completion. Generally means the stage at which works are sufficiently complete to be fit to hand over, albeit there may be minor defects or omissions.

Preliminaries. Work and materials necessary for the execution of building works, but not actually forming part of the completed works themselves. Examples are site huts, scaffolding, site clearance, plant and temporary lighting.

Prime cost. In broad terms, the cost to a contractor of executing building work, usually excluding overhead costs that are not exclusively referable to that work. Sometimes it is more exactly defined, eg in the JCT form of fixed-fee contract.

Prime cost contract. A contract where the price is fixed after the work is done by reference to the prime cost of the work. Synonym for cost-plus contract.

Prime cost sum. In a bill of quantities, the price placed against an item requiring the contractor to enter into a nominated sub-contract. The expression is to be distinguished from other uses of the expression prime cost; the tenuous connection is that under the usual nomination system the main contractor is, in respect of that work, paid whatever he (the main contractor) must pay the nominated sub-contractor. See p 36.

Programme. A diagramatic representation of the intended sequence of building operations. See p 57.

Prolongation. (*i*) Usually delay in the completion of the works that is the responsibility of the employer.
(*ii*) Synonym for prolongation costs.

Prolongation costs. Loss and expense caused to a contractor by reason of prolongation.

Provisional sum. (*i*) An item in a bill of quantities designed to approximately estimate the cost of work yet to be particularised. See p 37.
(*ii*) The expression is sometimes loosely used to describe any approximate estimate of the cost of building work.

Quantity surveyor. A surveyor whose principal function is to measure and value building work.

Relevant event. In the JCT form of contract, an event which entitles the contractor to an extension of time in which to complete the works.

Re-measurement contract. Hybrid between lump-sum contract and cost contract. See p 4.

Retention. The money deducted and retained by the employer from sums that would otherwise be due to the contractor, usually 5%. The retention fund is usually released as to half upon practical completion and as to the other half upon the architect's certificate of completion of making good defects. See p 22.

RIBA. Royal Institute of British Architects, whose headquarters are at 66 Portland Place, London W1 (not pronounced 'reeber', but RIBA).

RIBA Contract. The forerunner of the JCT contract, now sometimes used as a synonym for the JCT contract. See p 6.

Scott schedule. Familiar synonym for Official Referee's Schedule. See p 124.

Section 4 Summons. Summons issued by a defendant to court proceedings under the Arbitration Act 1950, s 4, seeking a stay of those proceedings so that the dispute may be referred to arbitration. See p 108.

Services. This expression is usually used to describe the installations that provide central heating, air conditioning, hot water, drainage, electric power, lifts, etc.

Small works agreement. Expression sometimes used to describe the agreement for minor building works issued by the JCT.

Snagging list. A list of minor defects and omissions usually prepared when works are nearing completion.

Specialist contractor. This expression is generally used to describe a sub-contractor (usually nominated) who is responsible for some specialised part of the works, such as services.

Specification. (*i*) Generally, any description of building works.

(*ii*) The expression is sometimes particularly used to describe a document containing special requirements as to the works, eg as to which British Standards the materials are to conform.

(*iii*) The expression is sometimes used to describe an informal or short document in lieu of a bill of quantities.

Spon's. A guide edited by Messrs Davis Belfield and Everest, Quantity Surveyors, to the cost of building works.

Structural engineer. An engineer whose principal responsibility is the load bearing structure of building works.

Subbie. Contractor's jargon for labour-only sub-contractor.

Sub-let. Synonym for sub-contract as a verb.

Substantial completion. That degree of completion which is ordinarily necessary for the contractor to recover anything under a lump-sum contract. It is usually a lesser degree of completion than practical completion or entire completion. See p 1.

Supervising officer. Creature of the JCT Local Authorities contracts, a person other than an architect who fulfills the function of certifier.

Target contract. There are various forms of complex arrangements whereby the method of calculation of the contractor's final entitlement depends upon whether the final cost of the works exceeds a pre-agreed target sum. The scheme is sometimes used where the employer and the contractor wish to share between them any saving in the anticipated cost of the works.

Tender. A formal written offer by a contractor to do work, usually (but not always) for a lump sum.

Turnkey contract. An expression sometimes used to describe a design and build contract where the contractor not only designs and builds the building but also designs and instals any plant necessary. The idea is that all the employer has to do is to turn the key to the front door and start using the building. The term, however, is not a term of art; *Cable (1956) Ltd* v *Hutcherson Ltd* (1969) 43 ALJR 321, High Court of Australia.

Uneconomic working. The disruptive effect upon the contractor of architect's instructions or interference via the employer. Often one head of a loss and expense claim by the contactor.

Valuation. This usually means the valuation of building work carried out by the quantity surveyor upon which the architect makes his interim certification of payment to the contractor, eg under clause 30.1.2 of the JCT contract.

Variation. This expression usually means a variation required by the employer or the architect on the employer's behalf. It rarely includes any unilateral change of plan by the contractor.

Work person. This expression has a precise definition under clauses 38.6.3 and 39.7.3 of the JCT contract and clause 35.6.3 and 36.7.3 of NSC/4.

Works. Shorthand for building works, meaning both the work and the materials required for the building.

Index

Building Contract Litigation

by Robert Fenwick Elliott

Supplement to First Edition

This supplement refers to some of the more important developments in this field over the past two years.

Page ix, second paragraph

There is now provision in the county court for summary judgment and interim payment.

Page xii: Table of Cases

Eames London Estates Ltd and Others v *North Hertfordshire District Council and Others* is now reported at (1980) 18 BLR 50.

Page xvii: References

There is now a supplement to the Fourth Edition of *Building Contracts*, by Donald Keating QC.

Page 14, first paragraph

The Association of Consultant Architects form of building agreement was published in 1982.

Pages 27–30: Implied terms

Much of the law concerning implied terms has now been codified by the Supply of Goods and Services Act 1982. Building contracts fall within Part I of the Act ('supply of goods') which applies to contracts made on or after 4 January 1983. Building contracts also fall within the scope of Part II of the Act ('supply of services') which has not, at the time of writing, been brought into operation.

Part I – Supply of goods

Section 2 of the Act implies terms about title etc that mirror s 12 of the Sale of Goods Act 1979.

Section 3 of the Act applies where there is a transfer of goods by

1

description, and there will almost always be such transfers in a building contract. The section provides for an implied condition (not merely a warranty) that the goods will correspond with their description, and this, accordingly, mirrors s 13 of the Sale of Goods Act 1979.

Section 4 of the Act deals with implied terms about quality or fitness. Section 4(1) apparently sweeps away all the existing case law on the implication of terms relating to fitness for purpose and materials. In substitution, the Act implies terms that reflect s 14 of the Sale of Goods Act 1979. The terms are:

  (a) by s 4(2), a condition that the goods are of merchantable quality;
  (b) by s 4(5), a condition that the goods are reasonably fit for any purpose expressly or impliedly made known to the transferor.

Section 5 of the Act applies to transfers by reference to sample, and so will sometimes be relevant to building contracts. The section mirrors s 15 of the Sale of Goods Act 1979.

Part I of the Act is not free from difficulty. First, the new terms as to correspondence with description, quality, fitness for purpose and correspondence with sample are all conditions and not warranties. Will this import a right of rejection for any breach, however trivial? There has in the past been a distinction between the stringent rules sometimes applied in sale of goods cases (see *Arcos Limited* v *E A Ronaasen and Son* [1933] AC 470), and the more pragmatic approach, tinged with considerations of reasonableness, which has ordinarily been applied in building cases (see *Wm Cory & Son Limited* v *Wingate Investments (London Colney) Limited* (1980) 17 BLR 104).

Secondly, there is provision under s 11(1) of the Act for the implied terms to be negatived or varied by express agreement, course of dealing or such usage as binds both parties to the contract. It is further provided by s 4(7) that an implied condition or warranty about quality or fitness for a particular purpose may be annexed by usage. How far will the court go in using these provisions to maintain the status quo? An educated guess might be that the Act will have little impact upon the way that building cases are decided.

Part II – Supply of services

Under this part of the Act terms will be implied that the buyers will carry out the service with reasonable care and skill (s 13); that where the time for performance is not fixed by the contract or course of dealing, the supplier will carry out the service within a reasonable time (s 14); and that where the consideration is not determined by the contract or course of dealing, the party contracting with the supplier will pay a reasonable charge (s 15).

Page 30: Design defects

The Canadian case of *Brunswick Construction* v *Nowlan* is probably no longer of much assistance regarding a contractors duty to warn the employer of obvious defects in the architect's design. It is now more pertinent to see this issue in terms of tortious duties than contractual duties, especially since the House of Lords decision in *Junior Books* v *Veitchi* [1983] AC 520.

It is worth recalling what Judge Fay QC had to say in *Eames* v *North Hertfordshire District Council* (1980) 18 BLR 50:

> 'During the hearing it was conceded that no case could be founded on [the sub-contractors] action in accepting the architect's instructions to design to three-quarters of a ton per square foot. The case made is that when it came to laying the foundations they knew or ought to have known that the ground was unsuitable and ought not to have proceeded. Mr May in the course of his cogent argument on their behalf submitted that they had discharged their duty by referring the matter to the architect and that they cannot be criticised for accepting the express instructions of the architect to proceed, especially since the designed footings had the blessing of the building inspector. I see the force of this argument, and I shall bear it in mind when I come to the question of contribution, but in my judgment it cannot remove liability from [the sub-contractors].'

Page 106: Order 29, Part II, second paragraph

Order 29, r 10 has now shown that it is capable of being used with significant effect in building cases. The present position can briefly be summarised as follows:

(a) It is now ordinarily advisable to include an Ord 29, r 10, application with practically every Ord 14 application in a building contract case.

(b) These Ord 14/Ord 29 applications are almost always best heard by an Official Referee, and this is so whether or not advantage is taken of the new provisions of Ord 26, r 2(1), allowing writs to be issued as Official Referees' business. In cases proceeding in the Queen's Bench corridor where the defendant has indicated that an Ord 14/Ord 29 application will be opposed it is appropriate for the outstanding Ord 14 summons to be transferred to an Official Referee together with the action itself. Failure on the part of the plaintiff to procure that transfer may lead to delay in that the Master in the Queen's Bench Division may make no other order on the special appointment save for transfer to an Official Referee.

(c) See page 120 as to the procedure on issue of summonses before the Official Referees. Note in particular that it is not now

possible to issue summonses in the Official Referees' corridor
without an estimate of the maximum hearing time, and an
indication as to whether counsel will be used. Lengthy
summonses are now heard on Fridays.

(d) Applications under Ord 29, r 10, need to be supported by
affidavit (Ord 29, r 10(3)). There is ordinarily no need for
separate affidavits under Ord 14 and Ord 29.

(e) The current practice of the Official Referees' Court is to cause
applications under Ord 29 to be returnable before an Official
Referee other than the Official Referee to whom the action has
been assigned. This practice reflects Ord 29, r 15, whereby it is
prohibited to communicate the fact of an order for interim
payment to the court at trial until all questions of liability and
quantum have been determined.

(f) It is particularly notable that the Court of Appeal held in *Fryer*
v *London Transport Executive* (1982) *The Times*, 4 December,
that the court may look at what payments have been made into
court in satisfaction, for the purpose of deciding what order to
make under Ord 29. It is further notable that successive
applications may be made under Ord 29 (Ord 29, r 10(5)). The
Official Referees have already shown that they are prepared to
make successive orders for interim payment in suitable cases.

Page 117: Additional ground

In *Turner* v *Fenton* [1982] 1 All ER 8, a stay was refused upon the
basis that the reputation of a professional man was at stake.

Page 118: Official Referees' Business, first paragraph

The definition of 'Official Referee' has been amended such that the
Lord Chancellor may appoint persons other than circuit judges: the
Rules of the Supreme Court (Amendment No 3) (1982 SI No 1786).
As matters presently stand, the anomaly remains that Official
Referees have circuit judge status notwithstanding that their
responsibilities are at the least on a par with other judges of the High
Court.

Page 118: Official Referees' Business, second paragraph

A fourth Official Referee has now been appointed: His Honour
Judge David Smout QC. His Clerk is Ms C Ball (extn 3181).

The Clerk to His Honour Judge Sir William Stabb QC is now
C Hawkshaw-Burn (01–405 7641 extn 3465) and the Rota Clerk is
now Mr R Carter (extn 3965). The Clerk to His Honour Judge John
Newey QC is now Ms BL Joy (extn 3456), and the Clerk to His

Honour Judge Lewis Hawser QC remains Mrs PM Bevan (extn 3457).

Page 119: Procedure on transfer to the Official Referee

Fundamental changes have been made to Ord 36 (which is the order dealing with Official Referees' business), by the Rules of the Supreme Court (Amendment No 2) (1982 SI No 1111). The major change is to permit appropriate cases to be treated as Official Referees' business from the time that the proceedings are issued.

Official Referees' business is now defined as any Chancery Division or Queen's Bench Division cause or matter:

(a) which involves a prolonged examination of documents or accounts or a technical scientific or local investigation such as could more conveniently be conducted by an Official Referee; or

(b) for which trial by an Official Referee is desirable in the interests of one or more of the parties on grounds of expedition, economy or convenience or otherwise.

For practical purposes this definition includes the overwhelming majority of litigation arising out of building contracts.

Ord 36 r 2(1) now reads as follows:

'Before the issue of a writ or originating summons by which Official Referees' business is to be begun, it may be marked in the top left hand corner with the words 'Official Referees business' and, on the issue of the writ or summons so marked, the cause or matter begun thereby shall be treated as Official Referees' business.'

The plaintiff's solicitor accordingly has a choice as to whether proceedings are to be treated from the outset as Official Referees' business. That is not, however, necessarily the end of the matter because proceedings in the Chancery Division or Queen's Bench Division may be transferred to be dealt with as Official Referees' business, either upon the application of any party by summons (r 3(1)) or upon the motion of the court itself (r 3(2)). Likewise, an Official Referee may of his own motion or on the application of any party order a cause or matter which is proceeding as Official Referees' business to be transferred to the Chancery Division or Queen's Bench Division if he considers that it may more appropriately be tried by a Master or Judge (r 3(3)).

No order for the transfer of proceedings shall be made by the court or an Official Referee under r 3 unless the parties have either had the opportunity of being heard on the issue or consented (r 3(4)).

The Official Referees do not adopt the Queen's Bench Division practice of waiting until pleadings are closed before giving directions. Rule 6(1) now provides that an application for directions (including an application for a fixed date for hearing) shall be made by the plaintiff to the Official Referee to whom the business has been allocated, within fourteen days of the giving by a defendant of notice of intention to defend, or the date of the order transferring the cause or matter whichever is the later.

Page 120: Official Referees' Court notes

The Official Referees' Court notes as to Ord 36 procedure has now been replaced by the following:

HIGH COURT OF JUSTICE
OFFICIAL REFEREES' BUSINESS
PROCEDURE (ORDER 36 R.S.C.)

1. Bring to Room 742 (Rota Clerk) the following:
   (a) Original Writ or Originating Summons and a Copy
   (b) Original Order (if any) referring the matter and a Copy
   (c) Praecipe E.26 (from Room 278), stamped £20 (unless the action has been previously set down for trial elsewhere and the fee was paid then. In this case, the document carrying the fee should be lodged with the Rota Clerk)
   (The matter will then be allocated to a particular Official Referee)
   (d) 2 copies of a Judge's Summons (Form S.1)
   (Suitable wording being; '...................... for further [or General] directions .... ')
   (e) Copy Pleadings (one set starting with a further copy of the Writ or Originating Summons)
2. All summonses will be issued by the Rota Clerk and should be lodged in duplicate. The following endorsement shall be completed before a date may be given:
   I/we estimate summons will not exceed ...... hrs ..... mins with/without counsel. Any change to be notified to Rota Clerk immediately.
3. All orders to be drawn up should be brought (in duplicate) with the summons carrying the endorsement, to the Clerk to the Official Referee to whom the matter has been allocated.

Pages 128–129: Pleadings, Note 2 to precedents

It is now necessary to plead statutory interest much more fully than was formerly the case. The substantive law is now contained in s 35A of the Supreme Court Act 1981 and the procedure is now set out in the Practice Note dated 24 February 1983.

In the ordinary case of interest sought under s 35A of the Supreme Court Act 1981, the Statement of Claim should now plead:
   (1) The date when the payment was due.
   (2) In respect of interest claimed from that date to the date of the

issue of the writ, the rate of interest claimed (which should not exceed the rate of interest on judgment debts—currently 12 per cent) and the amount of interest claimed.

(3) In respect of interest from the date of issue of the writ, a claim for further interest at the aforesaid rate to judgment or sooner payment. This should be shown as a daily rate to assist calculation when judgment is entered.

Page 130: Financing charges

The passage on financing charges must now be read subject to the replacement of s 3 of the Law Reform (Miscellaneous Provisions) Act 1934 by s 35A of the Supreme Court Act 1981.

Apart from this statutory change there has been further movement by the common law away from its old reluctance to fully compensate plaintiffs in interest terms. See in particular *Wadsworth* v *Lydall* [1981] 1 WLR 598; *Department of the Environment for Northern Ireland* v *Farrans (Construction) Limited* (1981) 19 BLR 1; and *Tate and Lyle* v *GLC* [1982] 1 WLR 149.

Page 144: Bremer Vulkan v South India Shipping

There has been further attention to the issue of delay in arbitration proceedings, and the House of Lords returned to the issue in *Paal Wilson & Co* v *Partenreederei* [1982] 3 WLR 1149. In summary, the present position seems to be as follows:

(a) Neither repudiation nor frustration are doctrines that can be used to strike out a dilatory claimant.

(b) The doctrine of abandonment can sometimes be applied where the claimant's conduct is such as to induce a reasonable belief that it intended to abandon the arbitration, and where the respondents do in fact believe that the claimant so intended and they themselves act accordingly; see *Andre et Compagnie S A* v *Marine Transocean Limited (The Splendid Sun)* [1981] 3 WLR 43.

It thus remains possible but very difficult for a respondent to see the end of lengthy arbitration proceedings.

Page 146: Arbitration, first paragraph

The Institution of Civil Engineers has now prepared a new Arbitration Procedure (1983) to be used with the ICE Conditions of Contract (5th Edition). This is a four page document setting out various procedural matters.

Page 158: Limitation of Actions

There have been further developments in the area of limitation in building cases. The House of Lords reviewed the position in respect of negligence claims in *Pirelli General Cable Works Limited* v *Oscar Faber & Partners* [1983] 2 WLR 6. In summary, the position is as follows:

(1) The commencement of the limitation period is no longer delayed merely because the defect had not been or could not reasonably have been discovered. Time begins to run when the damage actually occurs.

(2) Time does not begin to run again every time there is a change of ownership. Subsequent owners are no longer in any better position than their predecessors in title.

(3) The commencement of the limitation period *may* be postponed, at any rate in cases against local authorities, until such time as the damage causes danger to the health or safety of the occupants.

(4) The new fraudulent concealment provision (now deliberate concealment) in the Limitation Act 1980 is not confined to breach of contract cases, but extends to cases in tort.

© Oyez Longman Publishing Limited 1983
21/27 Lamb's Conduit Street
London WC1N 3NJ

ISBN 0 85120 767 7

Set in Times and Univers by
Kerrypress Ltd

and printed in Great Britain by

Dramrite Printers Limited, Southwark London SE1